westl

13 Steps to Blo

Ashwin Sanghi is counted among India's highest-selling English fiction authors. *13 Steps to Bloody Good Luck* is his foray into the world of non-fiction.

Till date Ashwin has written three independent novels, all bestsellers, including *The Rozabal Line*, *Chanakya's Chant* and *The Krishna Key*. In addition he has co-authored a crime thriller, *Private India*, along with James Patterson, the world's highest selling writer.

Ashwin's books have sold in the millions and have been translated into many languages. Ashwin was included by Forbes India in their Celebrity India 100 Rankings.

Ashwin is an entrepreneur by profession but writing is a passion that has evolved into a parallel career. When he isn't busy churning out bestsellers, he works for the MK Sanghi Group, which has business interests in automobiles, real estate, and engineering.

Ashwin was educated at the Cathedral & John Connon School, Mumbai, and St. Xavier's College, Mumbai. He holds a masters degree in business from the Yale School of Management.

Ashwin lives in Mumbai with his wife Anushika and his son Raghuvir.

Ashwin can be contacted on email at mail@ashwinsanghi.com, via his website at ashwinsanghi.com, through his Twitter handle @ashwinsanghi or on Facebook at facebook.com/shawnhaigins.

13 STEPS TO BLOODY GOOD LUCK

ASHWIN SANGHI

w

westland ltd
61, II Floor, Silverline Building, Alapakkam Main Road, Maduravoyal, Chennai 600 095
93, I Floor, Sham Lal Road, Daryaganj, New Delhi 110 002

First published by westland ltd, 2014

10 9 8 7 6 5

ISBN: 978-93-84030-57-5

Typeset by PrePSol Enterprises Pvt. Ltd.
Printed at Thomson Press (I) Ltd.

This little book is dedicated to my father, Mahendra Sanghi (the one who gave me the freedom to follow my dreams and shape my own luck).

Contents

I

The Three 'R's

Being a bestselling author is a wonderful feeling. My publisher loves me (almost unconditionally). My contracts get signed off (usually on my terms). My royalties allow me to live rather comfortably. At seminars, events and literature festivals, I am surrounded by readers and adoring fans. In that sense, I am an extremely lucky person.

But life wasn't quite always like that. I started writing my first novel at age thirty-six. Prior to that, I had not written anything longer than a couple of pages, not counting the extra-long answer sheets for my BA exams. (It was rumoured that examiners graded answer papers by weight.)

Three years later, when I was a bestselling author, many asked: 'Was it good luck or hard work?'

'I am a great believer in luck. The harder I work, the more of it I seem to have,' wrote Coleman Cox, a business author. I have always wondered whether Mr Cox was right. What if there is no such thing as good luck? What if one's success is purely related to hard work? Looking back at my journey, it would be wonderful to attribute my success as a writer to hard work. Who wouldn't like to take personal credit for success?

Observing the world around me though, I have come to the conclusion that Cox's theory is elegant—but wrong. My own success as an author has little to do with hard work or talent. Many individuals I have met work much harder than most of us, yet they sadly remain unsuccessful. I also know people who have achieved great heights with significantly less effort.

Many are the talented authors who toil over their manuscripts for years, often forgetting to eat or sleep in their quest for perfecting their masterpieces, which sadly, often remain unnoticed. We also see mass-market authors—like me—who are far less talented but whose bestsellers make millions.

We see the same phenomenon repeated in almost all fields of life: cinema, industry, banking, creative arts and even politics. One finds numerous examples of individuals who manage to attract much more than their 'fair' share of good luck. What explains it?

A Little Idea

At a recent literary event, a young lady asked: 'What are the factors that contributed to your success as an author?' My reply, probably unlike anything that she expected, was:

> After completing my first novel *The Rozabal Line*, I was in the process of making submissions to literary agents and publishers. After sending over a hundred letters, I was sorely disappointed when polite and not-so-polite rejections arrived. A year later, it was evident to me that no one was really interested in my work.
>
> I described my situation to a close family friend who was having dinner with my father. Taking a generous gulp of his third peg of Johnnie Walker Black Label, the gregarious Punjabi gentleman responded, 'In life, ninety-nine per cent is about good luck! Just remember that, son.'
>
> In a slightly argumentative tone I asked, 'But uncle, what about the balance one per cent? Surely that must be hard work or talent?'
>
> Laughing loudly, he declared triumphantly, 'The final one per cent? That's called *bloody good luck*, my boy! Simply keep at it and wait for your bloody good luck to kick in!'

The lasting impression of this story, which remained firmly etched in my grey cells, possibly explains my decision to share it with my audience at the literary event.

After the session concluded, the same lady hesitantly approached me in the lobby. 'Could I take a moment of your time sir?' she asked. Apparently, she had some issues with my anecdote.

'What is the point of working hard or developing one's skills if it all boils down to luck?' she asked. 'One may as well sit back and do nothing at all!'

She had a valid point.

Her argument compelled me to examine the concept of good luck more closely. As it turned out, I would spend several months agonizing over it.

Down the ages, humans have tried everything possible to improve their luck. Romans sacrificed animals before battles; Hindus used numerology, astrology and gems to improve their equation with the gods; parts of Africa used magic, witch doctors and spells to drive away bad luck; Europe used exorcisms, papal blessings and good luck charms; much of the world still resorts to prayer and rituals. The list is endless.

And that's precisely the problem.

Luck is associated with a variety of incomprehensible objects, superstitions and rituals, but is rarely analysed rationally. This gives good luck a bad rap. Thus, the world usually looks down on people who rely on luck.

Many months later, I was having a drink with a school friend, a well-established architect. Something he mentioned gave me an idea. It was almost a moment of enlightenment. I could barely restrain myself from blurting out the tagline of a mobile network company, 'What an idea, sirjee!'

This little book is simply about that idea, an idea about good luck.

The Napoleonic Characteristic

Consider an event from the life of Napoleon Bonaparte, one of the world's greatest military strategists:

> During a meeting, his subordinates informed Napoleon Bonaparte of a new general who was turning out to be extremely capable.
>
> The new man's bravery, skill, determination and organizational capabilities were outlined for Napoleon in great detail.
>
> Napoleon waved his hand impatiently. 'That's all very well,' said Napoleon. 'But tell me: Is he lucky?'

Napoleon's question may sound rather strange in our times, but he saw luck as a personal trait rather than an extraneous factor. A lucky person would succeed, even under adverse conditions. On the other hand, a capable and qualified general could prove to be disastrous on the battlefield—if he wasn't inherently lucky.

We know that it's possible to train oneself to be a good communicator, to be more organized, sociable or efficient. Many traits and personal attributes that may not be part of our nature can be developed through nurture. Can luck be similarly developed? Can one train oneself to be lucky?

So what was this conversation with my architect friend which led me to a fresh perspective? Let me repeat it for you.

Rain! Rain!

My friend mentioned that he was supervising the construction of a 'green' building in Mumbai. One of its main features was an advanced rainwater harvesting system.

'Mumbai's water requirement is around 4,200 million litres per day (mld). Of this, the Municipal Corporation supplies only 3,400 mld. That's a shortfall of 800 mld each day,' he explained.

'What's your point?' I asked, taking a sip of my favourite single malt—neat. (I avoided adding water in deference to my friend's concern about water scarcity.)

'Well, Mumbai receives around 2,200 millimetres of rainfall each year. If we could simply catch seventy per cent of this rainfall before it flows into drains or to the sea, we could eliminate our water deficit entirely,' he continued.

'What's your point?' you may well ask. Why am I discussing Mumbai's water woes in a book ostensibly about good luck?

The idea that struck me when my friend spoke was:

The rainfall, a free and universal resource, is available to the whole of Mumbai. Unfortunately, only some houses have rainwater-harvesting systems installed. These houses are able to catch, store and use the free rainwater; but houses without such systems are unable to do so.

Now consider this: What if life's opportunities are like rainfall, and we human beings are like houses? What if some of us have the ability to 'catch' opportunities as they fall, but others do not have the required 'infrastructure' to trap opportunities?

Isn't it possible that what my father's friend called 'one per cent bloody good luck' is simply the ability to catch the ninety-nine per cent when it presents itself?

That was the idea, sirjee!

Unfortunately, I was some distance away from sobriety during this moment of enlightenment and had to wait until the next morning to further dwell upon it.

Luck & Opportunity

Let's start by explaining a basic difference that is often misunderstood: the difference between luck and opportunity.

Like rainfall, most of the actual opportunities that come our way are not in our control. However, within a modest range, we can increase or decrease the number of opportunities coming our way through specific actions.

Opportunities can turn into good or bad luck depending upon their outcomes.

		Opportunities	
		Opportunity Availed	Opportunity Ignored
Outcomes	Opportunity Succeeds	Good Luck	Bad Luck
	Opportunity Fails	Bad Luck	Good Luck

Missing a flight for an important meeting could be bad luck. However, if that flight crashes, the missed flight could turn out to be very good luck indeed!

Bagging a large sales order could be good luck. However, if the customer goes bankrupt before settling his bills, the same order becomes bad luck.

In effect, *how we respond to opportunities and how the outcomes pan out determine whether we are lucky or not.*

Raise, Recognize, Respond

American financier Bernard Baruch once remarked, 'Millions saw the apple fall, but Newton asked why.'

Why did Newton ask why?

The ancient Greek scholar Archimedes saw the water level in his bathtub rise as he immersed himself. Shouting 'Eureka!' he leapt out of his tub and ran through the streets of Syracuse naked. Why had his discovery—a simple way of measuring an object's volume—not occurred to millions who had stepped into bathtubs? Consider a more recent example:

In 1984, a young lawyer sat in a Mississippi courtroom—as an observer—listening to a ten-year old tell a jury how she had been raped and beaten mercilessly.

He noticed the jurors' expressions. Many of them were crying. He wondered what would happen if the girl's father murdered his daughter's rapists out of despair, anger, frustration or revenge.

An idea for a story was born in the lawyer's mind. It took him another three years to actually write it. Twenty-eight publishers rejected his book before Wynwood Press—a little-known publisher—agreed to print five thousand copies.

The novel? *A Time To Kill.* The lawyer-turned-author was John Grisham, who went on to sell 275 million copies of his books, smashing many records along the way.

Several people attended this rape trial in Mississippi. Why did the idea of writing a great story present itself only to John Grisham? Or did the idea present itself to many but find a receptive mind only in Grisham? What specific innate qualities enabled Grisham to see the trial as an opportunity for a brilliant story?

In effect, my light bulb question was: If one needs a rainwater-harvesting system for harvesting rainwater, could there be an appropriate system to enable us to harvest opportunities?

Returning to our rainwater-harvesting example:

- Mumbai's annual rainfall is, for the most part, determined by nature.
- Mumbai can, however, increase its green cover, control its pollution and preserve its mangroves by which the city's rainfall will increase.
- Mumbai can increase paved surfaces—including rooftops and terraces—on which rain falls so as to increase the odds of catching it.
- Mumbai can provide an adequate network of pipes to ensure that such harvested rainwater is diverted away from the drainage system and into the sub soil, by which the water table will rise.
- This water can be extracted by bore wells when needed.
- Incidentally, rainwater-harvesting is compulsory and successful in Tamil Nadu, and the water table has measurably risen.

From this example, it should have become abundantly clear that our good luck is related to our ability to:

- Increase opportunities that come our way
- Recognize the valuable ones among them
- Respond to the recognized opportunities

The rest of this book will try to address these issues.

In the American world of basic education, *The Three 'R's* refer to the basic skills that all American elementary schools are expected to impart: *Readin', 'Riting, and 'Rithmetic.*

In the world of good luck harvesting too, we could call the basics The Three 'R's: *Raise, Recognize and Respond.*

RAISE	How can we raise the number of opportunities that come our way?
RECOGNIZE	How can we recognize these opportunities better?
RESPOND	How can we better respond to the recognized opportunities?

II

Attitude & Approach

Jean Cocteau, the French writer, artist and film director was once asked if he believed in luck. 'Of course,' he replied. 'How else do you explain the success of those you don't like?'

It's true, isn't it? When I am successful, it's because I worked for it, but when someone else is, he probably got lucky!

Common sense tells us that luck can't be controlled. It's related to chance and probability. According to Anthony Tjan, co-author of the *New York Times* bestseller *Heart, Smarts, Guts, and Luck*, there are three types of luck:

- Circumstantial Luck: I tag along with a friend to someone else's dinner party and get introduced to someone. We like each other, get romantically involved and eventually get married. Being at the right place at the right time made it possible. The *circumstances* made it happen.

- Constitutional Luck: Age, race, heritage, culture, or upbringing can predispose you to a certain outcome. For example, being promoted within a company because you are from the boss's hometown is *constitutional* luck.
- Dumb Luck: The sort of luck where one cannot analyse the cause and effect. Winning the lottery or finding a thousand rupee note on the pavement is simply *dumb* luck.

While constitutional luck and dumb luck are difficult to control, one can substantially improve the circumstantial luck in one's life.

How? Simply by raising the number of opportunities, recognizing the valuable ones and responding to the best ones.

But how exactly does one raise, recognize and respond? Let's examine a true-life story to understand the *how*:

Barnett Helzberg Jr., a successful businessman, had created a chain of extremely profitable jewellery stores with annual revenues above $300 million.

One fine day, while walking in front of the Plaza Hotel in New York, he heard a stranger addressed as 'Mr Buffet'.

Helzberg had heard of the legendary investor Warren Buffet, but had never seen him before. (In those times, Warren Buffet's face was not universally recognized.) Helzberg wondered whether the man stepping out of the hotel could be the same financial genius that Helzberg had read about.

Helzberg wanted to exit his business owing to his advancing age. Based upon some reports he had read, he knew the qualities that Buffet sought in an acquisition. Helzberg believed that his chain of jewellery stores could meet Buffet's criteria.

Deciding to take the bull by the horns, Helzberg walked up to the stranger and introduced himself. This turned out to be a great decision. The man was indeed Warren Buffet. A year later, he acquired Helzberg's business at an excellent valuation.

Lucky break for Helzberg? Sure. But the story illustrates many key attitudes and approaches needed to make that lucky break happen:

- Had Helzberg not been alert, he would have missed someone addressing a stranger as 'Mr Buffet'.
- Had Helzberg not read up about Buffet and his methods, he would have been unaware of the criteria by which Buffet evaluated acquisition opportunities.
- Had Helzberg not been intuitive, he would have ignored Buffet's name being called out. He would have walked on,

rationalizing that the odds of the person being Warren Buffet were simply too low.

- Had Helzberg been shy or fearful, he would have avoided going up to Buffet and introducing himself, and the opportunity would have been lost.

Thus, all the significant tools we need (to *raise* the number of opportunities that come our way, *recognize* the valuable ones among them and *respond* effectively to them) fall into two basic categories:

- *Attitude*: This refers to our way of thinking or feeling about someone or something. Our past successes, failures, interactions and experiences influence our attitudes, thus resulting in a tendency to instinctively favour or disfavour (sometimes erroneously).
- *Approach*: This refers to one's particular way of dealing with a situation or handling a challenge or task. Approach tends to be influenced by our education, work experience, training and skills.

Pretty much everything we do to make ourselves lucky or unlucky can be traced back to attitude and approach. Let me illustrate:

Richard Wiseman, a psychologist at the University of Hertfordshire, conducted a very interesting experiment to demonstrate that 'lucky' people are lucky because of their approach and attitude rather than chance.

Wiseman advertised in several newspapers and magazines requesting people who viewed themselves as exceptionally lucky or exceptionally unlucky to contact him for a research study.

Around four hundred people, aged between eighteen and eighty-four, volunteered. These men and women were drawn from all social and economic groups across varied career backgrounds: businessmen, teachers, factory workers, salesmen, secretaries, doctors, etc.

Wiseman asked each volunteer to count the number of photographs in identical newspapers they were given.

Members of the 'unlucky' group took around two minutes each to count the photographs, while members of the 'lucky' group took mere seconds. What could possibly explain the difference?

Wiseman had, rather sneakily, included a message on the newspaper's second page as a half-page ad in large and bold font. It said, 'Stop counting. There are 43 photographs in this newspaper.'

The message was right there for all to see, but the group that viewed themselves as unlucky were so anxious to get their counting done that they failed to spot the opportunity. They approached the task like a term paper, racing against the clock to get the paper finished. This prevented them from spotting the opportunity to stop counting!

On the other hand, the lucky group approached the task with less anxiety, greater optimism and in a far more relaxed frame of mind. They did not see the need to compete, and this relaxed attitude allowed them to observe beyond the immediate task at hand. This enabled them to spot the ad.

Jonathan Fields, author of *Uncertainty: Turning Fear and Doubt into Fuel for Brilliance*, says, 'Those who are doggedly attached to the idea they began with may well execute on that idea. And do it well and fast. But along the way, they often miss so many unanticipated possibilities, options, alternatives, and paths that would've taken them away from that linear focus on executing on the vision, and sent them back into a place of creative dissidence and uncertainty, but also very likely yielded something orders of magnitude better.'

What does this experiment reveal? Simply that luck is not entirely about chance; it's about the human ability to spot opportunities and make the most out of them. The tools that help us convert opportunities into luck relate to either attitude or approach.

In this chapter, we will consider how lucky people *think*, *react*, and *feel*. We will also learn what lucky people *do* differently. Thus, we'll consider both *attitude* and *approach*. So what exactly are these two terms I keep referring to? Let me illustrate with two—rather cheeky—tales.

The village panchayat was offering a bounty of a thousand rupees for every wolf captured alive in the neighbourhood.

Two friends Nilesh and Suresh decided to try their luck. For many days and nights they searched the surrounding forests and hills looking for wolves but with no success. One night, they could go no further and fell asleep in the forest, utterly exhausted.

In the middle of the night, they suddenly heard low growls. Both friends woke up with a start. They realized that they were surrounded by a pack of a dozen wolves.

Nilesh was terrified. The only thought in his head was that he was going to die that night. He nudged Suresh and whispered in a wavering voice, 'Are you thinking what I am thinking?'

Suresh looked at his friend and smiled. 'Yes,' he answered. 'I think we just made twelve thousand rupees.'

The difference between Nilesh and Suresh is *attitude*, not approach. They think and react differently to the situation that they are in. Now, the second story:

Two friends, Karun and Tarun, were in the temple courtyard, praying during an outdoor religious ceremony. Karun wondered whether smoking was allowed.

'Why don't you go ask the pujari for permission?' suggested Tarun. So Karun went up to the priest and asked, 'Panditji, may I smoke while I pray?'

But the priest turned down the idea. 'No beta, you cannot do that. It would be tantamount to disrespecting God.'

Karun returned to Tarun and repeated the priest's words. Tarun laughed and said, 'It was as expected. You asked the wrong question. Let me try.'

Tarun walked up to the priest, lit cigarette in hand, and asked, 'Panditji, would it be fine if I prayed while I had my smoke?'

The priest smiled and replied, 'By all means, beta. Any opportunity for prayer should always be availed of.'

The difference between Tarun and Karun was the way that they handled the task, their *approach*.

Approach is about action, the way that we *do* things, (as contrasted with attitude, which is more about how we *think or feel* about someone, something or a situation).

Now that we have understood the difference between attitude and approach, let's attempt to identify the approaches and attitudes that can help us harvest opportunities.

Comedian Milton Berle once said, 'If opportunity doesn't knock, build a door!' In the next chapter we shall try building a Luck Harvester instead of a door.

III

The Luck Harvester

While writing this book, I examined the lives of many successful and not-so-successful people to study what they had—or hadn't—done as pointers for lesser mortals like us.

After my initial research, I had a list of forty-seven points. I realized that many of them overlapped (so I merged them). I then reasoned that some were not really about attracting luck, but were actually about simply working better (so I discarded them). Finally, I was left with a list of just thirteen (so I further examined them).

Have you heard of *triskaidekaphobia*? It's a Greek word that means 'fear of the number thirteen'. Down the ages, there have been several reasons why the number thirteen has been considered unlucky. Theories include the absence of the thirteenth law from the Code of Hammurabi, the fact that Judas was the thirteenth to sit at the table of the Last Supper and that Friday the thirteenth began to be viewed as an unlucky day.

I shall not go into the details of those stories here but I started this book by saying, 'Good luck gets a bad rap due to superstitions.' It's precisely for this reason that I am happy to enunciate exactly thirteen principles to good luck given that it's almost oxymoronic.

These thirteen attitudes and approaches seem to be the 'magnets' that help lucky people raise their flow of opportunities, recognize valuable ones and respond to them effectively.

To the left of each of the thirteen suggestions are tick marks indicating whether the recommendation involves a change in attitude or approach (or both). Additional tick marks to the right of each point indicate how the change can help in raising, recognizing or responding to opportunities.

Without further ado, I now present the critical components of 'The Luck Harvester' or the thirteen steps to being bloody lucky.

1		NETWORK	Raise	✓
Attitude		*Lucky people grow and strengthen their network*	Recognize	
Approach	✓		Respond	✓

'Luck hates loneliness. It's almost impossible to be lucky alone,' says Philippe Gabilliet, Associate Professor in Psychology, Organizational Behaviour and Management at ESCP Europe. No man is an island. Just think about it. If you were to sit alone inside a room, cut off from the outside world, how would opportunities reach you?

A story from 1888 demonstrates how one's network is often vital in delivering good luck:

Much against his father's wishes, Asa Candler had avoided medical school, choosing instead to become a pharmacist in Atlanta.

John Pemberton, Asa's competitor in Atlanta, had been wounded in battle and had become addicted to morphine, which he often used to ease his pain.

Pemberton began experimenting with tonic concoctions containing Kola Nut and Damiana but his morphine addiction put him in severe financial distress.

Hearing about the situation from friends and neighbours, Asa Candler met Pemberton and negotiated to buy his latest tonic formula.

The purchase was for a tonic known as Coca-Cola.

Pemberton's concoction would make Asa Candler into a millionaire. However, what made that 'lucky' break possible? It was Candler's network. It was the network that informed Candler of Pemberton's financial distress, and which tipped him off to the possibilities of a new tonic.

Building and leveraging your network of family, friends, acquaintances and colleagues is critical. Tips and offers reach us via networks, competitors included.

To appreciate this point better, consider the story of a young Russian immigrant living in America:

Issur Danielovitch worked his way through college before attempting to enter show business. Living in a little room in Greenwich Village and working as a waiter, he managed to get just a few miniscule roles on Broadway.

When the Second World War began, Danielovitch was drafted into the US Navy, leaving behind a large circle of friends in New York. Among the many women he had kissed goodbye was a struggling actress Lauren Bacall.

While Danielovitch was serving in the Pacific, Lauren's career took off and she became a Hollywood star. When he returned to civilian life, Lauren got him to audition before one of her producers, which landed him a movie role.

Danielovitch eventually changed his screen name to something more American and was eventually listed among the greatest male screen legends in American film history by the American Film Institute. He received the Academy's Honorary Award for 'fifty years as a creative and moral force in the motion picture community.'

His screen name? Kirk Douglas.

Max Gunther's book *The Luck Factor: Why Some People Are Luckier Than Others And How You Can Become One of Them* carries a quote from Kirk Douglas himself: 'I guess I had some kind of talent. But if it hadn't been for this Lauren Bacall fluke, where would the talent have gone? Dozens of my friends back then had talent too, but you don't see their names in movies today… Your own luck depends on other people's luck. It's crazy!'

Not so crazy when one considers the concept of *Six Degrees of Separation*. It's a theory—formalized by Frigyes Karinthy and popularized via John Guare's play—that everyone and everything is six or fewer steps away.

In effect, I could connect to anyone else in the universe in a maximum of six steps through 'friend of a friend' introductions. What it also means is that any job opening, investment opportunity, joint venture, sales opportunity, romantic encounter, loan approval or marriage proposal is simply six degrees away!

Consider the sitar maestro Pandit Ravi Shankar's career to understand how the theory works:

Pandit Ravi Shankar was a music director with All India Radio (or AIR) from 1949 to 1956.

V.K. Narayana Menon, director of AIR New Delhi at the time, introduced Shankar to the internationally renowned violinist Yehudi Menuhin. Menuhin invited Shankar to perform in America.

As a result of his American tours, Shankar became friends with Richard Bock, founder of World Pacific Records. Shankar executed several recordings at Bock's studio.

The American rock band 'The Byrds' also used to record at the same studio. They ended up hearing Shankar's music. This led them to incorporate some of Shankar's music into their tracks.

The new sounds in The Byrds' music tracks came to the attention of George Harrison of the Beatles. Harrison soon visited India for six weeks to study the sitar under Ravi Shankar in Kashmir.

The Beatles went on to use the sitar in the 'Norwegian Wood' recording, thus creating a 'raga rock' trend in the west.

His association with The Beatles made Pandit Ravi Shankar the most famous Indian musician on the planet by 1966.

Six degrees of separation is much truer than we care to imagine. Ever heard about the chaos theory? More particularly, the butterfly effect? The name of the effect—coined by Edward Lorenz—is derived from the theoretical example of a hurricane's formation being determined by whether or not a distant butterfly had flapped its wings several weeks earlier! It's a perfect illustration of the extremely interconnected world that we live in.

Let's look at yet another story to help us appreciate the value of the network:

> Sardar Vallabhbhai Patel, the iron man of India, was known for his tough talking and no-nonsense approach. He is credited for having managed to merge 565 princely states into the Indian Union.
>
> Around the time of India's independence, it was debated if Indian Civil Service (ICS) officers should be replaced. They were seen as being overly loyal to the British authorities.
>
> Patel realized that governance in India would be severely impeded if capable bureaucrats were replaced. He drew a line of distinction between British ICS officers and Indian ICS officers.
>
> While the British officers were sent home, the Indian officers were asked to sign a commitment that they would serve the newly independent India with complete loyalty. Based upon that commitment, Patel allowed the Indian officers to continue administering India.
>
> The British-trained and sophisticated ICS lot had never thought much of Sardar, a dhoti-clad son of the soil. But that single decision transformed

Patel into a hero for the ICS and won him the undying loyalty of the Indian bureaucracy. In a single stroke, Patel had managed to create a huge network of capable administrators around him.

One ICS officer who would emerge as Patel's right hand man was V.P. Menon, the political adviser to the last Viceroy of India, Lord Louis Mountbatten.

After independence, Menon was appointed Secretary of the Ministry of the States, headed by Patel. Menon worked tirelessly under Patel for a herculean task: the integration of all the princely states into the union of India. Menon's presence was also vital in Hyderabad and Kashmir, which became law and order issues during integration.

Menon was even present at the famous meeting between Lord Mountbatten and Hanawant Singh, Maharaja of Jodhpur. After the Maharaja had reluctantly signed the instrument of accession to India and Mountbatten had left, the Maharaja threatened Menon with a .22 calibre pistol!

These were just some of the problems that Menon had to encounter while attempting to deliver on Sardar's agenda.

Sardar Patel was 'lucky' to have someone like Menon by his side, a man who would sweat and toil to implement his vision of a united India. But had he not protected the Indian ICS network, his 'luck' would never have kicked in.

Today many real-world relationships are being replaced by virtual relationships on social media platforms. It does not matter whether your network is real, virtual, or a combination of both. Being part of a network is critical for the flow of opportunities to happen. If one is active on Twitter, one has instant and direct access to Salman Khan, Narendra Modi, Sachin Tendulkar and Shahrukh Khan, amongst others. This was unimaginable a decade ago.

Each day, many upcoming authors contact me on Twitter, Facebook and LinkedIn, requesting me to read, review or recommend their work. Obviously, I can't accede to all requests owing to time constraints. However, I have occasionally acquiesced, particularly when the request came from a 'regular' on my social media network. One may call it the network effect!

Looking back at my journey in the publishing world, I am still amazed how the network effect was critical in producing my first lucky break:

After being rejected by most publishers, I had self-published my first novel via a US-based self-publishing platform. I soon realized that the platform was selling my books only via American online retail channels. My titles remained unavailable in India. My attempts to get published the traditional way in India had come to nought and I was at a dead end.

My mother knew someone at a publishing company and was happy to introduce us. Unfortunately that person had already decided to decline my work (like many others), but introduced me to Vivek Ahuja, who had worked for eighteen years with a large book distribution entity in India.

The incredibly helpful Vivek advised that I would have to import my books from the US and supply them on consignment basis to a few Indian distributors. Giving me a list of some key Indian distributors, he advised me to write to each of them individually, enclosing a copy of my book. One of the distributors on that list was East West Books.

One day, I received a call from a lady who introduced herself as Hemu Ramaiah. I did not know it at that time, but she was the founder of Landmark Book Stores and her company had just created a joint venture called Westland with East West Books.

Hemu said that she had loved *The Rozabal Line*, but it would be impossible to import the book from America and then expect to sell it in the Indian market at a reasonable price. Would I be willing to republish it in India? I jumped with joy at her question. I had been turned down by almost every publisher on the planet by then.

Hemu then introduced me to Gautam Padmanabhan, CEO of Westland (also my current publisher). We signed a contract two weeks later.

That's how my first novel got published. I sometimes wonder where I would have been if my mother had not known the contact at the publishing company; if that person had not known Vivek; if Vivek had not given me a list containing the East West name; if Hemu had not collaborated with East West; if Gautam had not been part of East West ... You get my drift? Opportunities flow through a network and we are much more interconnected than we care to imagine.

Many networks are available to us routinely: family, school friends, college alumni and colleagues at work. The important fact to note about lucky people is: They not only *strengthen* their existing networks, they also *grow* new ones.

Strengthening one's existing network is primarily about investing in relationships. If a friend needs a mutual introduction, do you oblige? If a colleague needs assistance on a project, do you help? If it's a relative's birthday, do you remember to wish her?

Cyrus Mistry, the current chairman of the Tata Group, was my classmate at Cathedral School. Cyrus was one of the naughtiest chaps in school, but everyone—teachers and students included—loved him. He could pull the chair away just as you were about to sit down and still offer you a genuinely friendly smile and hand to help you up. We celebrated our twenty-fifth year class reunion some years ago and there was a last-minute hitch with the venue. Cyrus, as usual, was quick to offer his own home as an alternative. It was his way of reaching out to all his school friends and teachers. That simple gesture is an excellent example of strengthening an existing network.

Remember, the ability to nurture a network is simple yet complicated because it involves dealing with human psychology.

Growing new networks is mostly about leveraging interactions. If you are seated next to a stranger on a flight, do you introduce yourself and try to strike a conversation? If you are invited to a friend's place for dinner, do you hang out with people you already know or do you attempt to meet new people? Chance encounters are often the routes through which opportunities manifest themselves. The following story illustrates my point:

Dileep Kumar was born in 1966. Unfortunately his father passed away when Dileep was just nine.

Musically inclined, Dileep was able to support his family by playing in various orchestras. After completing his education, he eventually moved into the world of advertising and began composing jingles.

One of the jingles that he composed was for Leo Coffee and it ended up bagging an award.

At a party hosted by the ad's producer Sharada Trilok, Dileep bumped into the famous film director Mani Ratnam who happened to be Sharada's cousin.

Some months later, Sharada called up Dileep to tell him that Mani Ratnam wanted to meet him. Mani Ratnam heard Dileep's compositions and was impressed enough to offer him a film.

Dileep Kumar was by then known as A.R. Rahman and that first film was *Roja*.

My father, Mahendra Sanghi, has always been a very sociable person, hosting dinners, attending multiple events and engagements regularly. In office, I always saw him dictating thank you notes, condolence messages, letters of congratulation and birthday and anniversary greetings. His secretaries had a tough time keeping up with his schedule. Many years later as a businessman, I realized that his legacy to me was the huge network of people he knew. There was almost no one who didn't know him!

Networks are not only important for creating opportunities; they are often also critical for responding to them. Take the case of N.R. Narayana Murthy, founder of Infosys:

'Always broke, Murthy always owed me money. We used to go for dinner and he would say, "I don't have money with me, you pay my share, I will return it to you later." For three years, I maintained a book of Murthy's debts to me. No, he never returned the money and I finally tore it up after our wedding. The amount was a little over four thousand rupees,' says Sudha Murthy, wife of N.R. Narayana Murthy.

Murthy married Sudha in 1978, while he was working with Patni Computers. Three years later, he decided to start Infosys along with six colleagues.

Murthy had the vision, but absolutely no capital. Unknown to him, Sudha had quietly saved ten thousand rupees, which she gave him as start-up capital when he needed it.

Infosys was initially set up in Pune. Sudha and Murthy's house (acquired with a joint loan) became the company's first office.

While Murthy ran Infosys, Sudha worked as a systems analyst with the Walchand Group to cover their household expenses. In fact, without Sudha Murthy, Infosys might never have started!

Journalist-writer Max Gunther sums it up beautifully: 'The bigger your web of friendly contacts, the better the odds in your favour. You cannot know what thunderbolt of good fortune is being prepared for you now by some distant engine of fate. You cannot know what complex interconnection of human relationships will guide the thunderbolt in your direction. But you can know, with certainty, that the probability of your getting hit is directly proportional to the number of people who know your name.'

<table>
<tr><td colspan="2">2</td><td rowspan="3">INTUITION
Lucky people listen to their intuition and develop it</td><td>Raise</td><td>✓</td></tr>
<tr><td>Attitude</td><td>✓</td><td>Recognize</td><td>✓</td></tr>
<tr><td>Approach</td><td></td><td>Respond</td><td>✓</td></tr>
</table>

All of us seem to have two voices inside us. The first is intuition, our 'inner wizard', which never shouts; it whispers. It tries to tell us what we should be doing and what will be good for us.

The second voice inside us is the 'inner critic', which shouts rather than whispers. Sending a steady stream of destructive thoughts directed towards us and others, it discourages us from acting in our own best interests.

Unfortunately, we usually end up listening to our inner critic rather than our inner wizard. Training oneself to ignore the inner critic and to listen to the inner wizard is what allows us to recognize opportunities for what they are.

Often, listening to one's intuition can be a lifesaver. Tom Justin, an American coach and speaker, once recounted a personal incident:

> 'I was flying frequently, sometimes three to four times a month, between Los Angeles and San Diego. I would take a morning flight, usually the same one, on Mondays. I much preferred flying to driving.

'One Sunday, though my day was filled with appointments with friends for brunch and a first date that I'd been trying to get for weeks and plenty of errands to run, I awoke and felt compelled to drive to San Diego that day.

'I mentally argued with that idea, especially since my date for dinner had been so hard to confirm. Nevertheless, I cancelled my day, my date and flight reservation and drove to San Diego on Sunday.

'The next morning, Pacific Southwest Airlines flight 182, my usual flight, was in a mid-air collision killing all aboard as well as others on the ground. On seeing the news on TV, I trembled at the thought of what had almost happened to me.'

Good luck that Justin wasn't on that flight? Sure. But the good luck only kicked in because he was willing to listen to his intuition!

Being intuitive does not mean disregarding reports, data analysis or other relevant information. One must absorb and *think* through all of those. The problem, however, is that most of us stop after thinking. We give ourselves no time to *feel*. Being intuitive is about thinking *and* feeling.

Noted turnaround specialist and former Burger King CEO James Adamson once revealed an interesting piece of information during an interview:

'Early in my career, when I was working with GAP, I was on a buying trip in the Far East. I picked GAP's first imported jeans, and bought far more than needed.

'To make a long story short, they sold out in less than thirty days of arrival. I thought I had bought a four-month supply!

'I had made a good decision on style and overbought based on my intuition. I just didn't know how good my intuition was!'

Even Conrad Hilton, the legendary founder of Hilton Hotels, claimed that his incredible success as a hotelier was often due to his lucky hunches:

Hilton submitted a sealed bid of $165,000 to buy a rundown Chicago hotel in a sealed bid auction.

The next morning, something didn't feel right. Acting on his intuition, he submitted another bid of $180,000.

When the bids were examined, Hilton's was the winning bid. The next highest offer? $179,800.

American talk show host, actress, producer and philanthropist Oprah Winfrey sums it up beautifully:

'Learning to trust your instincts, using your intuitive sense of what's best for you, is paramount for any lasting success. I've trusted the still, small voice of intuition my entire life. And the only time I've made mistakes is when I didn't listen. It's really more of a feeling than a voice—a whispery sensation that pulsates just beneath the surface of your being. All animals have it. We're the only creatures that deny and ignore it.

'How many times have you gone against your gut, only to find yourself at odds with the natural flow of things? We all get caught up in the business of doing, and sometimes lose our place in the flow. But the more we can tune in to our intuition, the better off we are.

'For all the major moves in my life—to Baltimore, to Chicago, to own my show, and to end it—I've trusted my instincts. I take in all the information I can gather. I listen to proposals, ideas, and advice. Then I go with my gut, what my heart feels most strongly.

'And I often tell friends: "When you don't know what to do, do nothing. Get quiet so you can hear the still, small voice, your inner GPS guiding you to true North."'

In his paper entitled *Best of Luck,* A.M. Murray says that a hunch should not be confused with an unfounded guess, wishful thinking or fear. Often, a good hunch is a conclusion based on real data, on facts observed and processed by your mind, even though you aren't necessarily conscious of them. Consider this example:

> When someone calls me on the phone and merely says 'Hello?' I instantly recognize her voice and greet her by name. I could spend hours trying to describe her voice, but it would be futile. Impossible.
>
> The truth is that my mind has stored thousands of data bits about that person: gender, language normally used in conversation, usual choice of greeting, depth, resonance, pitch and timbre of voice, pattern in calling time, pronunciation of specific words…
>
> I instantly 'know' who's calling even without having consciously or deliberately studied each individual element. Even if I wanted, I would be unable to describe each data bit that made my inference possible.
>
> But *not knowing consciously* does not mean *not knowing*!

When such an event happens, do we call it intuition? No. So why do we label other inferences in life (that are based on the very same process) as intuition? Einstein rightly said, 'A new idea comes suddenly and in a rather intuitive way, but intuition is nothing but the outcome of earlier intellectual experience.'

The need to listen to one's hunches is best summed up by an incident from the great composer Wolfgang Mozart's life:

A young musician asked Mozart, 'Herr Mozart, it has been suggested to me that I write a symphony. Would you be good enough to tell me how to go about it?'

Mozart thought for a moment and gently suggested, 'You are still too young to write symphonies. Why not try ballads first?'

'You wrote symphonies when you were ten years old,' argued the young man indignantly.

'Ah, yes, but I didn't ask how,' replied Mozart.

Absolutely. Mozart didn't ask how, because his inner voice had told him what to do. Mozart was willing to trust it rather than seek external affirmation.

Human beings have five senses: sight, smell, taste, touch, and hearing. But all of us also have a sixth sense. Some people call it common sense, others call it intuition. It's inside all of us, but some of us have succeeded in muzzling it.

So how does one develop intuition? Well, one has to find a way of learning to trust one's inner voice through baby steps. Start relying on your intuition for smaller decisions, then progress to bigger ones. R. P. Goenka, India's takeover king who acquired nine of India's finest companies within eight years, declared, 'My gut feeling is my only pathfinder.'

One of the greatest scientific minds, Albert Einstein, said, 'The intuitive mind is a sacred gift and the rational mind is a faithful servant. We have created a society that honours the servant and has forgotten the gift.'

3		**EXPERIMENT**	Raise	✓
Attitude	✓	***Lucky people are willing to try new things***	Recognize	
Approach			Respond	

TV actress Lucille Ball once remarked, 'I'd rather regret the things that I have done than the things that I've not done.' This pretty much sums up the attitude of lucky people. Their overall willingness to try new things simply increases the number of opportunities that come their way.

Satya Narayana Nadella is the Hyderabad-born son of an IAS officer who completed his basic education from Hyderabad Public School and Manipal Institute of Technology. He was named CEO of Microsoft in 2014. In a letter to all Microsoft employees, he said, 'Many who know me say that I am defined by my curiosity and thirst for learning. I buy more books than I can finish. I sign up for more online courses than I can complete. I fundamentally believe that if you are not learning new things, you stop doing great and useful things.'

Professor Wiseman (who ran the newspaper experiment described earlier) spoke to his subjects and found that many lucky individuals went to great lengths to induct variety into their routines.

One of Wiseman's subjects consciously took a different route to work each day. Yet another (who found himself speaking to the same set of people at parties he attended) imposed a 'colour rule' on himself. During a particular event, he would force himself to meet people who were dressed in specific colours. It could be black for a given event or red, blue, white or anything else for other events. This resulted in his chatting with people that he would never have otherwise interacted with.

Reminiscing about his schooldays, Mukesh Ambani once revealed that his father Dhirubhai had placed a premium on exposing his children to new experiences, activities and ideas:

> 'I remember my father never came to our school even once. Nevertheless, he was hugely interested in our all-round development for which he did some amazing things. Imagine this. In the mid-sixties, he put out a newspaper ad for a teacher, but specified that his responsibility would be non-academic; he would have to impart general knowledge.
>
> 'He interviewed several persons and selected Mahendrabhai Vyas who taught at the New Era School. Mahendrabhai came every evening and stayed until 6.30 or 7 pm. His brief was our all-round development. We played hockey, football and

different games, watched matches at Cooperage, travelled in buses and trains and explored different parts of Bombay. We went camping and stayed in a village for 10-15 days every year.

'These experiences have helped us a lot, but at that time, we were not very aware of all the learning that was going on.'

My friend, a real estate developer, took up golf out of sheer boredom. A couple of months later, he found himself playing with an expatriate who was seeking office space for his multinational company. My friend was able to strike a deal just two weeks later. The simple act of doing something new had opened up a new opportunity. This is amply demonstrated by a story of the great painter, Henri Matisse:

Matisse went to Paris to study law and started working as a court administrator in Le Cateau-Cambrésis after gaining his qualification.

Following an attack of appendicitis in 1889, he underwent a period of convalescence. His mother bought him some art supplies so that he could keep himself occupied even though Matisse had never painted till then.

Little did she realize that he would discover 'a kind of paradise' as he later described the experience.

He decided to become an artist, deeply disappointing his father by that decision.

Chetan Bhagat, India's bestselling novelist, is an IIT and IIM graduate. While working with Peregrine and Goldman Sachs in Hong Kong, he wrote his first book *Five Point Someone.* Imagine if he hadn't been willing to try writing that first book, he would never have gone on to sell the millions of copies that he eventually did.

Captain Gopinath, the founder of Air Deccan and the father of Indian low-cost aviation, writes in his autobiography *Simply Fly*:

> I reared cattle to sell milk, got in poultry farming, silkworm farming, then turned a motorcycle dealer, an Udipi hotel owner, a stock broker, irrigation equipment dealer, an agricultural consultant, a politician and finally an aviation entrepreneur—struggling, falling, rising, falling, rising again and taking off.

In effect, 'lucky' people are lucky because they expose themselves to more opportunities by being willing to do new things, meet new people or travel to new places. They are willing to work outside their comfort zones. The following business story from India illustrates how trying new things can work to one's advantage:

> In 1894, a young Parsi lawyer, fresh out of law school, went to Zanzibar to argue a case on a

client's behalf. Unfortunately, the case required him to twist facts to suit his client's story and the young man was unwilling to do so. He returned to India and gave up practising law.

While working at a pharmacy as the chemist's assistant in India, he noticed that all surgical tools were sourced from England through a long and tedious import route.

Taking a loan of three thousand rupees from a family friend, he began manufacturing scalpels, forceps, pincers, scissors and other surgical implements.

Unfortunately, the market only wanted 'Made in England' branded products, not Indian goods. He was forced to shut down the operation. However, by then he had understood the intricacies of working with metals and machines.

He went back to his benefactor for another loan. This time, it was for making locks.

His name was Ardeshir Godrej; the company he founded would eventually be known as Godrej & Boyce, which subsequently went on to manufacture safes, furniture, typewriters as well as a whole range of other consumer goods.

Tina Seelig, author of *What I Wish I Knew When I Was 20*, sums it up thus: 'Lucky people are open to novel opportunities and are willing to try things outside of their usual experiences. They're more inclined to pick up a book on an unfamiliar subject, to travel to less familiar destinations, and to interact with people who are different than themselves.'

Just look at the business success scripted by Jews, Marwaris, Sindhis and Gujaratis in alien countries. It is a clear illustration of the payoff that working outside one's comfort zone can bring.

Take my own example as a possible case study:

At thirty-five, having spent over twenty years running varied businesses for my family, I decided to write my first novel. I had never written anything longer than a couple of pages until then and was foolishly attempting to write a hundred thousand words.

My father was particularly concerned that I might cast aside my business avatar and become a fulltime writer. He probably had nightmarish visions of his MBA son wearing a *khadi kurta* and walking out of the family office with a jute *jhola* slung over his shoulder, ready to renounce the world on account of his passion.

I was far too realistic to do that. The odds of getting published were low, and the chance of earning royalties to sustain my living costs seemed next to impossible. I would have to continue working in the business for my keep. Writer Leo Rosten famously quipped: 'Money can't buy happiness, but neither can poverty.' The tug-of-war between business and writing—or wealth and poverty—would continue to plague me for the rest of my life.

One evening, over a drink with a close friend Sunil Dalal, I discussed my predicament. Sunil is a businessman who has successfully started, nurtured, and sold several large enterprises.

'I have garnered one important lesson from my business life,' he said, staring at me.

'What?' I asked.

'I have realized that the winner of the rat race is still a rat! Do you want to be just another rat all your life?'

His outburst had a profound impact on me and also led me to another observation: Sometimes we are so focused on winning the race that we do not realize that we may possibly be in the wrong race. My friend's observation enabled me to start taking my writing much more seriously.

I had once heard an Oxford-educated uncle tell a business partner in anger, 'You, sir, are a wolf in sheep's clothing!' Looking inward, I realized that I was also in disguise: a writer in a businessman's garb. I simply needed to come out of the closet! I needed to change the race that I was running.

There are several examples that illustrate the advantages of race-changing behaviour that worked:

Steve Jobs, the founder of Apple, started out with computers but went on to create the world's most successful animation company, Pixar. Upon returning to Apple many years later, he oversaw the creation of the iPod, iTunes music store, iPhone and iPad. He did not allow the commonly accepted description of computer hardware manufacturing to determine the boundaries within which he would operate. He changed his race often, and to dramatic effect.

Jeff Bezos, the founder of Amazon started out as an online retailer of books but then graduated to making Amazon into the biggest store on the web for almost everything. Not content with that, Bezos introduced the Kindle, coupled it with self-publishing platforms, and changed the face of publishing for ever.

Azim Premji, Chairman of Wipro Limited, inherited a company that manufactured hydrogenated vegetable oil. Thirteen years later, he changed the race by moving into manufacturing of computer hardware. Some years later, he once again changed the race by moving from hardware to software.

Jaithirth Rao—popularly known as Jerry Rao—worked with Citibank for twenty years before changing track in 1998 and starting the software company MphasiS. By 2000, Mphasis had risen to become one of the top ten Indian IT/

BPO companies. Eight years later, EDS acquired Mphasis. Two years later, Jerry again changed his race. He established Value and Budget Housing Corporation, an affordable housing venture aiming to alter the game in low cost housing.

Uday Kotak was born into a family of cotton traders, who commonly financed trades through bill discounting. Uday could easily have carried on the family tradition but he wondered what it would be like to be the financier-lender rather than the trader-borrower. This led to Kotak Mahindra Finance and, eventually, Kotak Mahindra Bank.

Many movie stars, including Jayalalithaa (Chief Minister of Tamil Nadu), the late N.T. Rama Rao (former Chief Minister of Andhra Pradesh), late Sunil Dutt (Member of Parliament for Congress Party), the late M.G. Ramachandran (Chief Minister of Tamil Nadu for three terms), Smriti Irani (TV soap star and politician) and countless others switched from cinema and entertainment to politics quite successfully.

A simple act of changing the race we are running often produces dramatically better results, but this requires openness to try new things. As of date, I am a well-established writer of historical and mythological thrillers. Am I not taking a substantial risk by writing this non-fiction self-help book? After all, this isn't my core strength, right?

Wrong! Changing the game makes us realize our inherent though latent strengths that can be better leveraged, thus making us better equipped to deal with new opportunities as they present themselves. Consider this incredible but true story from India:

A young man from Bengal, Abhas Ganguly, followed his actor brother to Mumbai to try his luck in Bollywood.

Abhas was able to get a few roles by leveraging some of his brother's contacts.

Four years after his first film, a celebrated music director noticed Abhas imitating a famous singer and suggested that Abhas should try playback singing.

Abhas Ganguly's screen name? Kishore Kumar.

Max Gunther says, 'The luckiest people I know haven't lived their lives in a straight line but in a zigzag. It's a mistake to get stuck on one track. You've got to be ready to jump off in a new direction when you see something good.'

Joking around with Sir Arthur Conan Doyle during a play rehearsal, a thin and wiry three-pound-a-week actor Charlie suggested that he and Sir Arthur should pool their incomes and take half each for the rest of their lives.

Though amused by the proposal, Sir Arthur Conan Doyle declined. Had he accepted the proposed deal that involved trying something new, he may have founded an enduring partnership with the soon-to-be-famous Charlie Chaplin.

4		**RISKS** *Lucky people take calculated risks, cut losses, and learn from mistakes*	Raise	
Attitude	✓		Recognize	✓
Approach	✓		Respond	✓

'Ratchet' is defined as 'a mechanism that engages the sloping teeth of a wheel or bar, permitting motion in one direction only.' Put simply, a ratchet is a device that permits a wheel to turn forward while preventing it from turning backwards. It safeguards the gains made by the wheel.

Lucky people organize their lives much like a ratchet. They remain aware that any risk taken can lead to loss or gain, but in the event of loss, they're not shy about admitting their mistakes. This makes it easy to cut losses in time. It also creates an environment for preventing a negative pattern.

Richard Branson, the founder of Virgin, says:

'Over the years, my colleagues and I have developed quite a reputation for risk-taking. It's true that we have been fearless about taking on new businesses, sectors and challenges even when the so-called experts told us that we did not know what we were doing.

'But while, to all appearances, we do have an unusually high tolerance for risk, our actions always spring from another principle: Always protect the downside. I think it should be a guideline for every entrepreneur or anyone involved in business ventures.

'For example, when we made the bold move of expanding from the music industry to the airline business, I set myself one condition: In our negotiations with Boeing, I stipulated that we could hand the planes back to them at the end of the first twelve months if people didn't like our business. That meant that I could see whether people liked the airline, but if it didn't work out, it wasn't going to bring everything else crashing down.'

Leonard Green, professor of entrepreneurship at Babson College, says, 'Entrepreneurs are not risk takers. They are *calculated* risk takers.' They take risks but they don't bet the farm. Understanding one's abilities and limitations is a key part of taking calculated risks. You may have the capital, but your health may be faltering. Could you really execute a project that needs your round-the-clock attention for the next three years, even though the opportunity may be exciting?

Anand Mahindra, Chairman of Mahindra Group, has been attempting to build an organization that can evaluate, incubate and scale up businesses continuously, even while failed experiments fall by the wayside. 'Measured risk-taking is at the heart of entrepreneurship,' he says. 'Whenever I have been unhappy about myself in my career, it has been because I have not taken an adequate and measured risk.'

The Satyam buyout by Mahindra illustrates the same approach. Anand Mahindra and Satyalingam Raju were both directors of the Indian School of Business. Mahindra floated the idea of a merger of their respective tech companies during one of their interactions, but Raju never got back. This turned out to be fortuitous because such a deal would have probably been very expensive for the Mahindra Group.

Some years later in 2009, Raju informed the bourses that he had been doctoring the company's financials. While others would have shied away, Mahindra saw it as an opportunity to strike. He spoke to Satyam's international customers: Microsoft, SAP and GE. The feedback was that all of Satyam's customers were rather happy with its services.

The decision was simple thereafter. Having secured a commitment from Vineet Nayar (CEO of Tech Mahindra) that he would be willing to devote the next few years to Satyam's turnaround, Mahindra decided to bid. He won the bid over stiff competition from L&T.

In financial year 2012-13, Mahindra Satyam gave the Mahindra Group a profit of Rs. 1,164 crores on revenues of Rs. 7,693 crores, thus casting aside any doubts whether Anand's decision had been the right one.

Rakesh Jhunjhunwala, the Pied Piper of Indian bourses, and probably the best example of calculated risk-taking, revealed once during an interview:

'My father was also interested in stocks. When I was young, he and his friends would drink in the evening and discuss the stock market. I found it very interesting and I got fascinated by stocks. I was self-taught.

'My father told me to do whatever I wanted in life but at least get professionally qualified. I was always a reasonably good student, so I took up chartered accountancy. In January 1985, I completed my CA.

'I then told my father that I wanted to enter the stock market. My father reacted by telling me not to ask him or any of his friends for money. He, however, told me that I could live in the house in

Mumbai and that if I did not do well in the market, I could always earn my livelihood as a chartered accountant. This sense of security really drove me in life.'

In other words, the downside was protected. If all failed, there was a backup plan. It was this knowledge that allowed Jhunjhunwala to play the stock market game in his style.

Sania Mirza, India's highest ranked tennis player, once said, 'I could add variation to my game, but I'm going to win matches only when I hit those winners. I enjoy hitting the ball as hard as I can. I enjoy taking risks. And I believe you always have to take risks.'

Essayist and playwright T.S. Eliot famously quipped, 'Only those who risk going too far can possibly find out how far one can go.' While some people follow the Eliot approach by actively seeking risk and being ready to bet everything on a seemingly bright opportunity, others take no risks at all because they are highly risk averse. Both sets of behaviour are dangerous.

Motivational speaker and author Shiv Khera says, 'Accepting responsibilities involves taking risks and being accountable, which is sometimes uncomfortable. Most people would rather stay in their comfort zones and live passive lives without accepting responsibilities. Accepting responsibilities involves taking calculated—not foolish—risks. It means evaluating all the pros and cons, then taking the most appropriate decision or action.'

Besides taking calculated risks, knowing when to cut losses and quit is another noticeable quality of lucky people. In his book *The Dip: A Little Book That Teaches You When to Quit (and When to Stick)*, author Seth Godin tells us that winners do quit, and that quitters do win.

Every new project, job, hobby or start-up begins with excitement and fun. It then tends to get more difficult and much less fun, until it hits a low point. Often you may find yourself asking if the goal is even worth the effort.

According to Godin, it's possible that you're in one of two situations: a *dip* or a *cul-de-sac*. A dip is a temporary setback, one that can be overcome if you keep pushing. But maybe it's really a cul-de-sac (the French term for a dead end), which will never get better, no matter how hard you try. What sets lucky people apart from others? They have developed the ability to distinguish between a dip and a cul-de-sac and to escape dead ends quickly, while staying focused and motivated when it really counts.

Godin tells us that winners quit fast, quit often, and quit without guilt—until they commit themselves to beating the right dip for the right reasons. Once they realize that they are dealing with a dip, not a cul-de-sac, they persevere like crazy to beat it.

The ratchet effect, however, is not only about taking calculated risks and quitting in time, but also about taking concrete steps to prevent bad luck in the future. Most of us call such steps 'learning from mistakes'.

The problem with the usual notion of learning from mistakes is that most of us build negative conditioning rather than simply understanding what aspect of our attitude or approach was wrong. For those who have read *Alice in Wonderland* by Lewis Carroll, Alice and the Mad Hatter have a conversation that illustrates exactly what I mean:

> Alice: Where I come from, people study what they are not good at in order to be able to do what they are good at.
>
> Mad Hatter: We only go around in circles in Wonderland, but we always end up where we started. Would you mind explaining yourself?
>
> Alice: Well, grown-ups tell us to find out what we did wrong, and never do it again.
>
> Mad Hatter: That's odd! It seems to me that in order to find out about something, you have to study it. And when you study it, you should become better at it. Why should you want to become better at something and then never do it again?

Why indeed! Let me narrate a relatively recent business example to illustrate how lucky people distinguish between a dip and cul-de-sac and how they prevent future mistakes:

Tata Motors decided to establish a car manufacturing facility in Singur, West Bengal. The state government acquired 997 acres of farmland to enable the Tatas to build the plant there. Due to subsequent local and political opposition the project went into limbo.

Ratan Tata had to take a decision whether to stay on and wait for the storm to pass or to exit West Bengal. In effect, he had to decide whether the Singur agitation was a dip or a cul-de-sac.

In 2008 (the year in which the first car was meant to roll out from the plant) the Tatas announced their decision to pull out from West Bengal, thus signalling that Singur was a cul-de-sac, an irresolvable predicament. This was followed by an announcement that they would establish a new plant at Sanand, Gujarat.

The new factory in Gujarat came up in a record 14 months as against the 28 months taken in West Bengal.

The Tatas also learned from the mistakes made in West Bengal. In West Bengal, the government had acquired extremely fertile land at a pittance by using the provisions of an 1894 land acquisition act. Thus the local opposition was understandable. Unfortunately there was trouble initially in Gujarat too.

Immediately after the Gujarat deal was announced, the Gujarat Industrial Development

Corporation (GIDC) notified six villages for acquisition in Sanand. Farmers opposed the deal, believing that the government was attempting to take away their land for free. Around 3,000 of them staged protests.

Desirous of not repeating the Singur mistakes, the Gujarat government brought the protesting farmers to the negotiating table, explained that it was not trying to acquire their land for free and declared an acquisition price that was a multiple of the market price.

The opposition dissolved and all farmers willingly cooperated with the government's acquisition.

One may question Tata's decision to pull out from West Bengal but the story emphasizes the importance of distinguishing between a dip and a cul-de-sac. Had Tata not pulled out from West Bengal, the subsequent success in Gujarat may never have happened. Also, if Singur hadn't happened, the Sanand land deal might not have been handled as efficiently as it was.

Ratan Tata took a calculated risk by setting up Singur, then cut his losses by exiting Singur. Learning from his mistakes at Singur, he avoided repeating them at Sanand.

5		**POSITIVITY**	Raise	✓
Attitude	✓	***Lucky people stay positive, persevere and cultivate a thick skin***	Recognize	
Approach			Respond	✓

The Secret by Rhonda Byrne emphasizes the immense power of human thought. At the core of *The Secret* is the theory that 'thoughts become things'. If you believe something strongly enough, the universe makes it happen.

Byrne's view is based on the metaphysical belief that our minds emit and receive energy from the universe. Byrne compares the brain to a transmission tower. Unlike a physical magnet where opposites attract, your mind pulls energy of the same frequency due to the law of attraction. Therefore, whatever signal you send into the universe via your thoughts, you receive in return.

At a fundamental level, my key takeaway from *The Secret* was the necessity of having a positive attitude in life. There are several instances that reinforce this idea:

Indira Gandhi remained India's Prime Minister for almost fifteen years. Though born in an illustrious and well-connected family, her father was always short of money.

Her academic life suffered due to her mother's illness. She also saw her parents go to prison several times during the freedom struggle.

One may agree or disagree with Indira Gandhi's politics, but one cannot ignore her positive attitude in approaching problems in her life.

Initially, she had to challenge the power centres within the Congress Party who dismissed her as a *goongi gudiya* (or mute doll). She eventually succeeded in establishing herself as the nucleus of the Congress Party.

She showed her strength and resolve during the Bangladesh war which went her way even though the US was firmly opposed to India's intervention.

Her decision to impose a state of emergency resulted in a crushing defeat for her party during subsequent general elections, but she bounced back a couple of years later with renewed vigour. She had foreseen the self-destruction of the Janata Party.

Indira Gandhi is known to have joked, 'I was, like Joan of Arc, perpetually being burned at the stake!'

Lesser mortals would have crumbled, but she didn't. It is said that fortune knocks but once, but misfortune has much more patience. If we are positive—and patient—the universe seems to send good luck our way.

Mark Murphy, the author of *Hiring For Attitude*, carried out a research project that involved tracking 20,000 newly hired employees. He found that forty-six per cent of them failed within eighteen months. But even more surprising than the failure rate was the fact that when new employees failed, eighty-nine per cent of the time their failure was due to attitudinal reasons; lack of skill was a factor only eleven per cent of the time! Just imagine how important a positive attitude is.

Adopting a positive attitude often requires us to stop associating with persons with negative attitudes. There exists a breed of individuals who excel in playing the role of victim. In fact, they almost enjoy failure because it gives them a chance to moan about their latest perceived victimization. The sooner one eschews the company of negative individuals, the better it is for one's positivity.

Keep in mind, though, that a positive attitude is of no use without persistence. Thomas Edison, the inventor of the electric light bulb, is known to have said, 'I have not failed. I have just found ten thousand ways that won't work.' Persistence thus seems to be a key factor in attracting good luck.

In the world of Indian business, the two names that are always mentioned in hushed tones of reverence are those of Tata and Birla. But here's something about them to think about:

Jamsetji Tata is remembered today as the pioneer who built the Taj Mahal Hotel in Mumbai and the man who envisioned the steel industry and hydro-electric power for India. But few remember that in 1863, Jamsetji tried establishing an Indian bank in England and brought the Tata firm to the verge of bankruptcy. His honesty and determination won him several friends in England who were happy to appoint him liquidator at a fixed salary. It was this allowance that enabled him to survive. Luckily, the ensuing Abyssinian War resulted in a spike in demand for Indian cotton and Jamsetji went on to acquire a rundown mill in Chinchpokli, thus managing a turnaround in the Tata fortunes.

Similarly, Ghanshyamdas Birla also found himself in deep trouble in 1919. He had fought with his own family as well as the British authorities to establish a jute mill. The First World War broke out just before his machinery order could be executed. He had projected that he would spend six thousand rupees per loom. Because of the war, the price shot up to sixteen thousand rupees per loom, almost three times the initial capital outlay. He still went ahead! The subsequent growth of the Birla fortunes is well documented.

You will agree that both the Tata and Birla stories are perfect examples of positive attitude coupled with persistence.

The construction of the Brooklyn Bridge that links Manhattan Island to Brooklyn is usually considered a story of bad luck, because everything that could possibly go wrong actually did. You should decide for yourself whether it was a story of bad luck or good luck:

> In 1863, an engineer John Roebling thought that a bridge connecting Manhattan Island to Brooklyn was possible. Across the world, bridge builders had told him that it simply could not be done.
>
> Roebling convinced his son, Washington, who was also an engineer. The father-son team developed the design and formalized the construction process. Soon, a crew began work on the bridge.
>
> Construction had been in progress for only a few months when a serious accident on site resulted in John Roebling's death. Seriously injured, Washington was left paralysed, unable to walk or talk due to brain damage.
>
> Since the father and son were the only ones who knew the details, design and execution plan of the bridge, it was assumed that the project would have to be shelved.
>
> Washington still wanted to complete the project and an idea struck him as he lay in hospital. All he could move was one finger, so he touched his wife's arm with that single finger, tapping out code to communicate with her.

He would continue tapping for the next thirteen years until the bridge that could never be built was built! That's the power of persistence.

If one really wants to get an idea of how persistence attracts luck, here's an important list of events in an American politician's life.

1831 – Lost his job
1832 – Defeated in run for Illinois State Legislature
1833 – Failed in business
1835 – Sweetheart died
1836 – Had nervous breakdown
1838 – Defeated in run for Illinois House Speaker
1843 – Defeated in run for nomination for US Congress
1848 – Lost re-nomination
1849 – Rejected for land officer position
1854 – Defeated in run for US Senate
1856 – Defeated in run for nomination for Vice President
1858 – Again defeated in run for US Senate
1860 – Elected President of the US

It's the story of Abraham Lincoln, the sixteenth president of the United States of America.

Do you see the point? Thomas Edison rightly observed that our greatest weakness lies in giving up. 'Many of life's failures are people who did not realize how close they were to success when they gave up. The most certain way to succeed is always to try just one more time,' said Edison. In effect, good luck seems to be largely a matter of hanging on after others have let go.

I have always maintained that the bestselling writers of our times are not necessarily the best writers. They are simply the ones who were obstinate enough to continue trying while other writers (probably much more talented) gave up.

We all know that the odds of getting heads when tossing a coin is 50:50. That's the theoretical model. But practically, someone who tosses the coin a thousand times will have many more heads (and tails) in absolute terms than someone who tosses it a hundred times. George Bernard Shaw astutely said, 'When I was young, I observed that nine out of ten things I did were failures. So I did ten times more work.'

In 2013, I was invited to speak at a college in Kolkata. After the event, I asked the taxi driver to show me a few interesting spots in the city. He took me to the Bondel Gate area on Sridhar Roy Road.

'There's an interesting temple inside, sir,' he said, pointing to an unassuming entrance in an ordinary building. Entering, I saw a massive green throne nestling a portrait of Bollywood superstar Amitabh Bachchan (along with a pair of his shoes) inside a modest room. A Brahmin was busy performing *aarti* of the portrait while reciting verses from a little prayer book (called the *Amitabh Chaleesa*) that was also being sold outside.

Amused by the temple, I began to wonder whether our current mythological figures—Krishna or Rama—had also started out simply as great men who began to be worshipped due to their great deeds. Then another thought struck me:

Many of Amitabh's early films did not do very well. He subsequently enjoyed a period of immense stardom coinciding with his image of 'the angry young man'.

In the early eighties, he was injured on a movie set and remained in hospital for many months, often on the verge of death.

He then entered politics, but resigned three years later owing to the unfortunate Bofors scandal that would plague him for many years.

He returned to films, but all his movies seemed to fail at the box office. He went on to incorporate a company, ABCL, which went belly-up.

The year 2000 was a turning point when he began hosting *Kaun Banega Crorepati* on TV. The show went on to become a massive hit, and was followed by several hit movies.

Today, he is the most enduring and successful icon that Bollywood has ever produced.

If there is ever a lifetime that resembles a roller coaster ride, it is Amitabh Bachchan's. He has seen success and failure in abundance, but keeps bouncing back after every failure. He is the embodiment of Thoreau's view that all misfortune is but a stepping-stone to fortune.

George Patton, the general who led American troops into the Mediterranean during the Second World War, correctly observed, 'Success is how high you bounce when you hit bottom.'

The Japanese believe in a good luck totem: the *Daruma Doll*. Legend has it that a monk, Daruma, sat in meditation for so long that his limbs eventually vanished. Thus the Daruma Doll is egg-shaped and bears a rather heavy and rounded bottom. What is the remarkable feature about the Daruma Doll? When you knock it down, it manages to stand up again. It doesn't matter how hard you knock it, or how many times you knock it, it somehow always manages to rise again. Amitabh Bachchan is like that Daruma Doll!

What was the inherent quality that enabled Mr Bachchan (and so many others) to remain inspired even in adversity? Wasn't their good luck related to the fact that they continued in their quest, even in the face of trying circumstances? Wasn't their good luck related to the fact that they could recognize opportunities at times when lesser mortals would have simply given up?

Henry Ford said, 'Failure is simply the opportunity to begin again, this time more intelligently.' The examples cited above confirm Ford's view.

Robert Schuller, the American televangelist, explained it wonderfully. He said, 'Failure doesn't mean you are a failure. It just means you haven't succeeded yet.' It is thus evident that while some lucky people succeed because they are so destined, most succeed because they are determined. If one is persistent, Lady Luck is left with no alternative but to manifest herself eventually.

Often, struggle is the best teacher and paves the way for future successes. The story of the butterfly's cocoon illustrates this point vividly:

A boy found a butterfly's cocoon in his garden one day. Next day, he noticed that a small opening had appeared. For several hours, he watched patiently while the butterfly struggled to force itself out through the little hole. Then it stopped struggling, almost as if it could go no further.

Deciding to help the butterfly, the boy used a pair of scissors to snip the remaining bit of the cocoon and the butterfly emerged easily.

Something was rather strange though. The butterfly had a swollen body and shrivelled wings. The boy continued to wait expectantly, hoping that at any moment the butterfly's wings would expand to support its body and the body would contract.

Neither event happened. In fact, the butterfly spent the rest of its life crawling around with a swollen body and deformed wings, never able to fly.

What the boy in his kindness and haste did not understand was that the restricting cocoon and the resultant struggle required for the butterfly to get out are Nature's way of forcing fluid from the butterfly's body into its wings so that it is ready for flight after achieving freedom from the cocoon.

Sometimes struggles are exactly what we need in life.

Ralph Waldo Emerson, the American essayist, wrote, 'Our greatest glory is not in never failing, but in rising up every time we fail.' He also said, 'A hero is no braver than an ordinary man, but he is braver five minutes longer.'

Being positive and persistent often also requires the ability to cultivate a thick skin. This prevents criticism and negative feedback from pulling us down:

Samuel Johnson, the English critic, poet and essayist, is believed to have once told a young writer, 'Your manuscript is both good and original; but the parts that are good are not original, and the parts that are original are not good.' Ouch!

All of us have faced, and will face, hurtful situations. I sent my first (self-published) novel to a professional reviewer, because newspapers and magazines were unwilling to read and review self-published books. The last line of her review made me want to die. 'A torturous, circuitous tale that could easily have stopped on page eight!' Ouch! Ouch!

Next year, my novel was launched in India by my current publisher. The very first review I received was from *The Hindu Literary Review*. I was extremely nervous, as my publisher had warned that a piece of thriller fiction was unlikely to garner a great review.

'A provocative, clever and radiant line of theology, Sanghi suggests that the cult of Mary Magdalene has its true inspiration in the trinity of the Indian sacred feminine, thereby outthinking and out-conspiring Dan Brown,' is what *The Hindu* wrote.

Why am I revealing this to you? Simply to show that had I allowed myself to be affected by that first review, I would never have made it to the second.

After many years of countless analysts predicting that Reliance was a bubble that would eventually burst, its founder Dhirubhai Ambani had a smile on his face when he said to a magazine, 'I am the bubble that burst!' It's the perfect example of cultivating a thick skin.

A famous newscaster said 'A successful man is one who can lay a firm foundation with the bricks that others have thrown at him.' One simply cannot run one's life based upon other people's views and opinions. And whenever one does anything meaningful, one must be equally prepared for criticism or praise. 'One learns to ignore criticism by first learning to ignore applause,' said Robert Brault, quite correctly.

6		**ALERTNESS**	Raise	
Attitude		***Lucky people find ways to remain calm and thus alert***	Recognize	✓
Approach	✓		Respond	✓

Let me start this section with a small but witty story about the great scientist Sir Isaac Newton:

> Newton once invited a friend to dinner and then forgot about it. When the friend arrived, he found the scientist deep in meditation.
>
> Knowing that the scientist should not be disturbed while in contemplation, the friend sat down quietly and waited.
>
> Sometime later, dinner for one was brought on a tray. However, Newton continued to remain in meditation. Pulling up a chair and without disturbing Newton, the friend silently ate the dinner.
>
> Later, Newton came out of his contemplative state, looked with some confusion at the empty dishes, and said, 'If it weren't for the proof before my eyes, I could have sworn that I had not yet dined.'

Most lucky people have understood that calming the mind is a key method to increase alertness. Many years ago I visited Igatpuri (near Nashik) to attend a *Vipassana* meditation camp. The course participants had to meditate for over ten hours daily and maintain complete silence throughout the ten-day stay. In the evenings we would hear videotaped lectures by Shri S.N. Goenka, the founder of the movement. It was possibly the only human voice we heard during our entire stay. One of his lectures was about taming a wild elephant:

> The method used to tame wild elephants in ancient times was to tie the captured beast to a firm post with a strong rope.
>
> The unhappy animal would scream, stamp and throw a fit, usually for several days.
>
> Eventually, the elephant would realize that it could not escape. At this point it would settle down. The trainer could now begin to feed and handle it with some measure of safety.
>
> After some time, the trainer would be able to dispense with the rope and post entirely.
>
> According to proponents of Vipassana, the human mind is like a wild elephant; mindfulness is the rope; and meditation is the fixed post.
>
> Meditation and mindfulness can tame the mind, much like the post and rope can tame the beast.

Lucky people find their own unique ways to tame their minds. Hence they are better able to deal with situations in their lives. Vipassana proponents always stress that if you are insulted by someone and get angry, the result is not the abuser's fault. It is your fault because you choose to react. In similar vein, self-help author Wayne Dyer said, 'How people treat you is their karma; how you react is yours.'

Let me narrate a small story about the importance of remaining neutral, almost meditative while facing life's situations:

A farmer in China used an old horse to till his fields. One day, the horse escaped into the hills. When his neighbours sympathized with him over his bad luck, the farmer replied, 'Bad luck? Good luck? Who knows?'

A week later, the horse returned with a herd of wild horses. This time, the neighbours congratulated him on his good luck. His reply was, 'Good luck? Bad luck? Who knows?'

Then, when the farmer's son was attempting to tame one of the wild horses, he fell off its back and broke his leg. Everyone thought this very bad luck. Not the farmer, whose only reaction was, 'Bad luck? Good luck? Who knows?'

Some weeks later, the army marched into the village and conscripted every able-bodied youth.

But since the farmer's son had a broken leg, they let him off.

Now was that good luck or bad luck? Who knows?

Those who worry create inner disturbance; this mental upheaval does not allow them to take the best of decisions. Remaining calm and relaxed even in trying circumstances is a trait of lucky people. A story from the Zen archives illustrates this point beautifully:

After winning several archery competitions, a young and rather arrogant champion challenged a Zen master who was famous for his archery skills.

The young archer displayed his amazing prowess by hitting a distant bull's eye on his very first attempt, and then proceeding to split the first arrow with his second. 'Let's see if you can do better,' he said haughtily to the wise old Zen master.

Unaffected by the young man's wizardry and arrogance, the master did not draw his bow. Instead, he motioned for the young archer to follow him up a mountain.

Curious about the old fellow's plans, the champion followed the master high into the mountain until they reached a deep chasm bridged by a rather flimsy and extremely shaky log.

Calmly stepping out, the old master walked to

the middle of the perilous bridge, picked a distant tree as his intended target, drew his bow, and shot a clean, direct arrow into it. 'Now it is your turn,' he said to the young archer, stepping nimbly from the bridge to terra firma.

The young man stared with panic into the seemingly bottomless abyss. He could not force himself to take a single step on the delicate log, much less shoot a target.

'You have much skill with your bow,' said the Zen master quietly. 'Unfortunately you have little skill in calming the mind that lets loose the shot.'

The Zen master had learned the art of staying calm while continuing to be alert. Often it is this alertness that allows us to spot opportunities when they arise. Consider the case of the world's biggest fast food company, McDonald's:

The brothers Richard and Maurice McDonald had established McDonald's, a fast food restaurant. The restaurant used Castle Multimixers to make milkshakes. Ray Kroc supplied these machines to McDonald's among others.

When Ray noticed that the McDonald brothers had purchased eight Multimixers in a very short period, he visited their San Bernardino restaurant to investigate.

Seeing their efficient operation convinced Ray that their scientific restaurant processes could be converted into a national franchising opportunity.

He quickly offered to become a franchising agent for the brothers and opened McDonald's Inc.'s very first restaurant in Des Plaines, Illinois.

He eventually bought out the company from the brothers in 1961 for $2.7 million. By 2012, McDonald's Corporation had annual revenues of $27.5 billion, profits of $5.5 billion and more than 34,000 stores globally.

Good luck for Ray Kroc? Yes. But his good luck only happened because he was alert to a sudden spike in the sales of Castle Multimixers!

Sometimes, good luck comes in the form of unpleasant experiences. One may call it 'good luck in disguise'. If we are alert, we are able to see through the disguise. Take the example of cricket maestro Sachin Tendulkar, who recounted an incident that changed his life:

As a student, Sachin used to visit his aunt after school for lunch, then hurry to the grounds for matches organized by his coach Ramakant Achrekar.

One day, Sachin decided to skip his training and joined a friend at Wankhede Stadium to watch a match between the English-medium and Marathimedium students of his school Shardashram. By chance Sachin's coach was also present there.

Sachin, carrying his tiffin box, went to greet Achrekar. The coach knew that Sachin had skipped his match, but pretending to be ignorant of the fact, asked Sachin how he had performed. Sachin truthfully replied that he had skipped his game in order to cheer for his school team.

The next moment, Sachin's tiffin box flew out of his hand. Ramakant Achrekar had delivered a tight, stinging slap across his face. 'You don't have to be here to cheer others. Play in such a way that others cheer you,' the coach sternly told him.

According to Sachin, that particular slap was a life-changing moment for him. It was the day that he began to take his training very seriously.

If it had been someone other than Sachin, the slap could have put him off cricket for the rest of his life, but in Sachin's case, it didn't. Was the slap anything other than a stroke of good luck for Sachin?

Thomas Edison rightly observed, 'We often miss opportunity because it's dressed in overalls and looks like work.' The slap was simply a nudge to work harder.

The Persian poet and philosopher Rumi once asked, 'If you are irritated by every rub, how will you be polished?' Differentiating between hard knocks in life and opportunity's knocks is sometimes difficult. Good luck is all around us, but we are often unable to recognize it because it could appear in disguise and we are not alert to this fact.

Before George Bernard Shaw became famous, one of his plays was consistently turned down by a producer. After Shaw achieved success, the producer suddenly cabled an offer to stage the rejected work. Shaw cabled back: 'Better never than late.' The producer had simply not been adequately alert to the fact that Shaw was a rising star.

Henri Matisse's painting 'Le Bateau' hung upside down in the Museum of Modern Art, New York, for 47 days in 1961 before anyone noticed! Even if just 0.01 per cent of the 116,000 gallery's visitors in that period had been alert, over a dozen should have reported this blunder.

Quite often, people whose very existence depends on opportunity recognition (venture capitalists, for instance), lose out on significant opportunities because they are not adequately alert.

A venture capital company, Bessemer Venture Partners, has published an 'anti-portfolio' on its website. It's a list of the great companies that they missed out investing in. The list includes Apple, eBay, Google, Federal Express, Intel and PayPal!

Probably Bessemer is able to talk about these missed opportunities with dignity because, on an average, they have scored more hits than misses.

And that's precisely what one needs to work towards for generating good luck—garnering more hits than misses over the long run.

The sad truth is that lost opportunities are better recognized when they are leaving rather than when they are coming. Mark Twain jokingly quipped, 'I was seldom able to see an opportunity until it had ceased to be one.'

Take another example, that of Nestlé milk chocolate. It would never have been created but for the fact that its creator, Daniel Peter was alert to the fact that his neighbour knew something that Peter didn't:

A successful confectioner, Daniel Peter was looking for a way to add milk to his chocolate to give it a soft and creamy texture.

Unfortunately, Peter was experiencing a fundamental problem: how was one to successfully extract water from milk while retaining all its key properties? Try as he might, he was unable to figure out a solution.

Peter's neighbour and friend Henri Nestlé was a pharmacist. Henri had managed to develop a formula named 'farine lactée' for children who could not breastfeed. That formula was based on milk and cereal prepared through a special baking process.

In 1875, Peter and Nestlé successfully combined

their respective products (chocolate and condensed milk) to create a wonderful product that came to be known as milk chocolate.

Stressing the importance of staying open and alert to maximize one's luck quotient, author Tina Seelig says, 'Lucky people take advantage of chance occurrences that come their way. Instead of going through life on cruise control, they pay attention to what's happening around them and, therefore, are able to extract greater value from each situation.'

Let me end this section by narrating a funny incident from the life of the great playwright William Shakespeare who remained extremely alert, particularly when it came to women who caught his fancy.

Actor and theatre owner Richard Burbage was playing the lead in Shakespeare's play Richard III.

A few minutes before a performance, Shakespeare overheard Burbage flirting with a young lady who lived near the playhouse. They set up a rendezvous at her house after the performance. 'Announce yourself as Richard III,' she suggested playfully to Burbage.

Shakespeare slipped out of the theatre before the performance ended and quickly walked over to the woman's house. Announcing himself as Richard III, he was admitted into her bedroom.

After completing his play, Burbage arrived later for his romantic encounter and sent a message that 'Richard III' was at the door.

Shakespeare laughed. He asked the maid to deliver the following message to Burbage: 'William the Conqueror came before Richard III.'

And these, my friends, are the rewards for being alert!

7		SITUATIONS	Raise	✓
Attitude	✓	***Lucky people make the best of bad situations***	Recognize	✓
Approach	✓		Respond	✓

I was once invited to address the students of IIM, Ahmedabad. One of the other panellists was Anu Aga, former chairperson of Thermax Ltd. She began her talk by summing up the experiences of her life. She left me stunned:

Aga was born in 1942 in an upper middle-class Parsi family in Mumbai. A degree in Economics, post-graduation in medical and psychiatric social work and a Fulbright scholarship later, she married a bright Harvard scholar, Rohinton Aga. Tragedy struck just after their daughter's marriage.

Rohinton passed away in 1996 suddenly after a heart attack and Aga found herself ill-prepared to take his place as chairperson of Thermax, an engineering company established by Aga's father A. S. Bathena three decades earlier.

Thermax had been managed extraordinarily well by Rohinton. Anu had been happy to simply take care of human resources. She was now expected to run the entire company and win back the fast diminishing trust of shareholders. She decided to persevere in the hope that she would one day be able to hand over the reins to her son Kurush.

Unfortunately, much more misfortune was in store for her. Her mother-in-law passed away; then Kurush (just twenty-five at the time) and the hope for Thermax's future, died in a road accident.

Three debilitating deaths would be more than enough to finish off any ordinary person entirely, but Aga took over the management of Thermax. There was no alternative.

At the time, Thermax's growth curve dipped and share prices plummeted from Rs. 400 to Rs. 36. An anonymous letter from a shareholder accusing her of letting him down forced her to take stock of the situation.

'I realized I wasn't capable but was only pretending to run the business,' she said. Losing no time, she inducted a foreign consultant to restructure the company and develop an action plan. This move revived the fortunes of Thermax.

As of 2013 Thermax served 75 countries and had annual revenues of around fifty billion rupees. Aga was soon listed by Forbes among the forty richest Indians by net worth. After retiring from Thermax, she took to social work, and in 2010 the Indian government awarded her a Padma Shri for Social Work. She was nominated to the Rajya Sabha in 2012.

The stories of Atal Behari Vajpayee (India's tenth Prime Minister) and Narendra Modi (India's fifteenth Prime Minister) illustrate what I mean by making the best of a bad situation:

In 1996, Vajpayee became Prime Minister but his government lasted only thirteen days. He became PM once again in 1998 but his government only lasted thirteen months. Many people jumped to the conclusion that the number thirteen had proved unlucky for Vajpayee. The truth was far from it. The two short stints in government made Vajpayee realize the importance of building a sound coalition of allies. He became PM once again in 1999 and served a full term precisely because of the skills he acquired in managing allies.

Narendra Modi was ridiculed as a *chaiwala*—a mere tea-seller—by some of his political opponents.

Modi used the barb to his fullest advantage. He effectively marketed his own humble origins as contrasted with the privileged upbringing of his rivals. During the election campaign his managers organized meetings at tea stalls and called them *Chai Pe Charcha* (discussions over tea). During these sessions, Modi would interact with his audiences via video conferencing. A single barb was turned into a deadly weapon by Narendra Modi thus resulting in his becoming the fifteenth Prime Minister of India.

Thus lucky people are simply those who use every bad situation to the best of their abilities. British Indian novelist Salman Rushdie's example reinforces this point:

Salman Rushdie's fourth novel, *The Satanic Verses,* published in 1988, became the centre of a major controversy, provoking protests from Muslims in several countries, some violent. Death threats were made against him, including a *fatwa* (or legal decree) issued in 1989 by Ayatollah Khomeini, the supreme leader of Iran.

Provided round-the-clock protection by the British government, Rushdie went into hiding for the next ten years. He was constantly under threat, but even during these troubled times, he decided to maintain a journal, a record of his life on the run.

> In 2012, he published *Joseph Anton: A Memoir*, an account of his years in hiding. (Joseph Anton was Rushdie's pseudonym during those difficult years.)
>
> Rushdie had used his years on the run to complete yet another literary project!

Or consider Martha Stewart, America's domestic lifestyle queen, who was imprisoned for insider trading charges:

> In 2004, Martha Stewart's world came crashing down. After a media circus and a much-followed trial, Martha was found guilty of conspiracy, obstruction of justice and lying to federal investigators about a stock sale. She spent five months in prison and six under house arrest.
>
> Today, almost every bookstore prominently carries her book *The Martha Rules*. Containing ten rules, it is a road map for entrepreneurs to create their own successful businesses. Martha started writing this book in prison as a project to help fellow inmates who sought her advice.
>
> Since then, Martha Stewart has added 7,000 new products to her name, published her 71st book, runs four magazines and has four TV shows on Hallmark Channel.

Dr Gita Piramal, Managing Editor of *The Smart Manager*, once received an autobiographical note from Raibahadur Mohan Singh Oberoi, the legendary founder of Oberoi Hotels, recounting his early days of struggle:

'Plague in those days was a terrible killer and people naturally dreaded an epidemic, which often wiped out villages. In this mood of depression, I saw an advertisement in the local newspaper for the post of a junior clerk in a government office. With twenty-five rupees in my pocket, which my mother had given me, I left for Shimla to appear for the examination.

'One day, as I was passing the Hotel Cecil, I suddenly had the urge to go in and try my luck. Those were the days when this hotel was one of India's leading hotels, high class and elegant. It was owned by the line of Associated Hotels of India. As I entered, I found the manager himself in the foyer. I did not know who he was, but one becomes bold in the face of difficulties. I had nothing to lose, so I went up and asked if I could have a job in the hotel.

'The manager was a kindly English gentleman named D.W. Grove. I was given the post of billing clerk at forty rupees a month.'

Imagine walking penniless off the street into a high-society establishment and asking for a job whilst surrounded by death! That's precisely what got the Oberoi story moving: A simple case of making the best of a lousy situation.

The life stories of some of the 'luckiest' people reveal that most of them thrived under conditions of adversity:

Beethoven composed his best-known masterpieces after he became deaf.

Sir Walter Raleigh wrote *History of the World* during his thirteen years in prison.

Columbus endured most adverse conditions during his expedition to America and no one would have blamed him for turning back. But had he turned back, no one would have remembered Christopher Columbus.

The Discovery of India was written by Jawaharlal Nehru during his imprisonment in Ahmednagar Fort from 1942 to 1946.

Martin Luther translated the Holy Bible while confined in the Castle of Wartburg.

Hellen Keller wrote twelve books, several articles, and delivered hundreds of lectures in over forty countries in spite of being born deaf and blind. Keller is known to have said 'Keep your face to the sun and you will never see the shadows.'

With a sentence of death hanging over him, Dante wrote the *Divine Comedy* during twenty years of exile.

Oscar Wilde famously quipped, 'We are all in the gutter, but some of us are looking at the stars.'

One's ability to look at the stars seems to be the key factor in driving oneself to use bad times to one's advantage. Consider:

Jan Koum, a very poor immigrant from Ukraine, regularly queued up with his mother for food stamps.

Brian Acton lost a fortune in the dotcom bust and was rejected for jobs by Twitter and Facebook.

Becoming close friends while working at Yahoo! Jan and Brian left the company in 2007 and took a year off, exploring South America and playing Ultimate Frisbee even though they were unemployed.

Two years later, they proceeded to spawn a new messaging service.

Five years later, Facebook acquired their messaging service, WhatsApp, for a stock-and-cash deal worth US $19 billion!

The WhatsApp story is the perfect illustration of the 'Dalai Lama Factor' at work. What is the Dalai Lama Factor, you ask? Well, the Dalai Lama came up with a brilliant insight. He said, 'Remember that not getting what you want is sometimes a wonderful stroke of luck.' If the WhatsApp founders had been 'blessed' with steady jobs they may possibly not have felt the urge to take the entrepreneurial plunge.

Here's another example of the Dalai Lama Factor at work:

Avul Pakir specialized in aeronautical engineering and it was his dream to become a fighter pilot. He received two interview calls. He ranked ninth (among twenty-five final candidates) in his interview with the Indian Air Force in Dehradun, but was not selected as there were only eight vacancies.

Hence he was forced to join the second organization: the Directorate of Technical Development and Production (DTDP) at the Defence Ministry in Delhi.

Who was this candidate? Avul Pakir Jainulabdeen Abdul Kalam, more commonly known as A.P.J. Abdul Kalam, the Missile Man of India, and India's eleventh President.

Not getting what he wanted had put A.P.J. Abdul Kalam into a trajectory that would ultimately shower him with far greater rewards.

Let's temporarily return to my efforts to get published:

After multiple rejections, I decided to attempt self-publication. I propped up my sagging sentiments by recalling that Margaret Mitchell's *Gone With The Wind* was rejected thirty-eight times before it was published. Anne Frank's *The Diary of a Young Girl* received fifteen rejections. Stephen King's *Carrie* was turned down thirty times before it was published. *Harry Potter and the Sorcerer's Stone* was rejected a dozen times and J.K. Rowling was sarcastically told not to consider quitting her day job. I convinced myself that I too would have to go through trial by fire, which was part of the game.

While self-publishing is an opportunity to get your work out into the market without the approval of a traditional publisher, the odds of being successful are exceedingly low. According to Google's advanced algorithms, over 129 million books have been published in modern history. Around a million books are added each year in the US alone, of which around half are self-published. On an average, each self-published title will sell 57 copies during its lifetime (mostly to the authors' families and friends, I imagine). The truth is that most writers can write books faster than publishers can write cheques. Tough odds indeed.

But I was lucky. My self-publishing adventure led to my work being accepted by a traditional publisher and eventually hitting the Indian bestseller lists. That led to two more bestsellers in the next six years as well as a partnership with the world's leading thriller writer, James Patterson.

While in conference with my publisher, I once joked about the numerous rejections I had received.

'You've heard the Latin phrase *Cogito Ergo Sum*?' my publisher Gautam asked.

'Sure. Descartes said it. "I think, therefore I am,"' I replied.

'In your case the phrase should be modified to, "I sank, therefore I swam!" Count your failures as your biggest blessings. It was your decision to make stepping-stones out of stumbling blocks,' he philosophized.

Ajay Piramal, Chairman of India's Piramal Group, was only 29 when his father died suddenly in New York. His elder brother took the reins, but died of cancer just five years later, leaving behind a young widow and three children. Prior to that, another brother had decided to quit the family business. In parallel, a one year long textile strike spearheaded by Datta Samant had brought the textile industry to ruin; Morarjee Mills, the family's mainstay, was incurring massive losses.

Piramal recounts that he survived those troubled times by reminding himself of one particular story:

One night a man dreamt that he was walking along the beach with God. Scenes from his life flashed in the sky as they walked. For each scene, the man noticed two sets of footprints (his and God's) in the sand.

On careful observation, he noticed that there was only one set of footprints at the saddest times of his life. He asked: God, why did You abandon me when I needed You most?'

> God whispered, 'My son, I was carrying you during the saddest times of your life; hence your footprints are missing.'

Lucky people seem to create an alternative support system—faith, prayer, hobbies, meditation, friends—to tide over their bad phases and are thus able to use such periods to the best of their abilities.

Let me end this section with BBC interviewer John Simpson's anecdote about Nelson Mandela:

> My warmest memory comes from a visit Mandela made to my old college at Cambridge.
>
> Mandela is an excellent speaker, with a real feeling for his audience and what they want to hear; again, I suppose this comes from that deeply personal sympathy for each individual he meets.
>
> 'I am very nervous about speaking here,' he announced. 'For three reasons. First, I am an old-age pensioner.'
>
> A faint titter of amusement went round the hall, but uncertainly: was he joking? Or was he simply being self-deprecating?
>
> 'Secondly, because I am unemployed.' A slightly louder, more confident laugh; he had stepped down as President not long before.
>
> 'And thirdly, because I have a very *baaaaad* criminal record.'

The laughter then nearly broke the stained-glass windows.

The 'unemployed old-age pensioner with a criminal record' had succeeded in destroying apartheid in South Africa by spending twenty-seven years in prison! *That's* called making the best of a bad situation!

8		**CONFIDENCE**	Raise	✓
Attitude	✓	***Lucky people develop their confidence and communicate***	Recognize	
Approach	✓		Respond	✓

Awkward and shy during my teenage years and always overweight, I remember attending parties with the nagging fear of not knowing anyone, of having to sit alone in a corner nursing a drink. I inevitably ended up doing precisely that.

During my last few years in school, some teachers forced me into elocution, debates and dramatics. Though I was initially nervous, my self-confidence increased with every successive competition. I eventually reached a stage where I actively sought opportunities to speak (and had to be gently reminded to shut up).

So what is the solution to acquiring confidence? It's simple. Conquer fear.

Overcoming fear—of any sort—allows one to open up to the flow of opportunities. Bertrand Russel, the British philosopher and mathematician, observed, 'To conquer fear is the beginning of wisdom.'

In the book *Maximize Your Potential: Grow Your Expertise, Take Bold Risks & Build an Incredible Career*, Michael Schwalbe of Stanford University explains why fear gets in the way of luck. It involves the mental duel that occurs each day between risk-taking and the fear of failure.

Citing the work of psychologists Daniel Gilbert and Timothy Wilson, Schwalbe explains the 'impact bias'. The impact bias is our tendency to greatly overestimate the intensity and extent of our emotional reactions. The net result of this bias? We expect failures to be more painful than they actually are, so we fear them more than we need to.

Consider legendary investor Warren Buffet, who had a fear of public speaking:

> Billionaire investor Warren Buffett was petrified of public speaking. He would pick his college classes carefully to ensure that he would not have to address the class.
>
> Buffet joined a public speaking course but never attended any of the sessions. 'I lost my nerve,' he said in an interview later.
>
> He wasn't alone. Countless famous people, including Bruce Willis, Tiger Woods, Julia Roberts, Anthony Quinn, Jimmy Stewart (even Sir Isaac Newton!) had issues with public speaking.

At twenty-one, Buffett started his investment career and realized that he simply had to overcome his fear of public speaking. Buffett signed up for a Dale Carnegie course with many like him who were scared of 'getting up and saying our names.'

Fast forward to the annual meeting of Berkshire Hathaway's shareholders. Each year, more than 35,000 shareholders descend upon Omaha. It is but obvious that Buffet is the star attraction. Buffet not only speaks, but manages to sing, dance and pose for photographs!

My point: it *is* possible to overcome fear and shyness. By doing so, we become much more capable of seizing opportunities.

In *Julius Ceasar*, William Shakespeare wrote:

There is a tide in the affairs of men,
Which, taken at the flood, leads on to fortune;
Omitted, all the voyage of their life
Is bound in shallows and in miseries.

It is often fear or shyness that prevents us from seizing the moment; from setting sail at the precise moment when the tide is just right. And as Shakespeare says, the tide waits for no one.

Another reason for fear can be explained by the 'Monte Carlo Fallacy'. The Monte Carlo Fallacy (or Gambler's Fallacy) is the mistaken belief that if something happens more frequently than normal during some period, then it will happen less frequently in the future, presumably as a means of balancing nature. So if someone tossing a coin got six consecutive heads, one is lulled into believing that the next result will be a tail. The truth is that the odds haven't changed. The odds of the next toss are still 50:50. The problem with the Monte Carlo Fallacy is that someone who has had a spate of good luck automatically tends to believe that his next venture will be unlucky or vice-versa. In effect, the Monte Carlo Fallacy reinforces irrational behaviour.

Building one's confidence means conquering fear. One of India's top Bollywood actors Shahrukh Khan (or SRK) has found a unique method to consume his fear. He talks about using fear as a propelling force to fuel one's pursuits instead of trying to overcome it. Addressing a conference of industrialists, SRK said:

> 'Successful people are almost never able to pinpoint what it was that made them so. Success just happens, really. So, talking about how to become successful is a waste of time. So let me tell you, very honestly, whatever happened to me, happened because I'm really scared of failure. I don't want as much to succeed, as much as I don't want to fail.
>
> 'So when I got a chance to act in films, it wasn't out of any creative desire that I signed my films, it was purely out of the fear of failure and poverty. Most of them were discards of other actors and the producers could not find anyone else to do them.

'*Deewana*, my first hit, was actually discarded by an actor called Arman Kohli. *Baazigar* was rejected by Salman Khan. *Darr* was negated by Aamir Khan. I did them all just to make sure I was working. The timing or something was right, and that made it happen that I became a big star.'

What SRK omits to mention is that he *did* have to overcome his fears to opt out of the Master's degree in Mass Communications that he was pursuing at the time. He *did* have to overcome his fear to shift from New Delhi to Mumbai. And he *did* have to overcome fear to pursue the directors who would give him his first roles.

One of the results of conquering fear and gaining confidence is improved communication skills. Consider the story of the French writer, historian and philosopher Voltaire, who was able to save himself because of his confidence *and* his communication:

When Voltaire was living in exile in London, popular feelings against the French were running high in England.

One day as he was walking on the street, he was surrounded by an angry mob yelling, 'Hang him! Hang the Frenchman!'

Turning to face the mob, Voltaire said, 'Men of England! You wish to kill me because I am a

Frenchman. Am I not punished enough in not being born an Englishman?'

This clever and tactful speech pleased the mob immensely. They actually cheered him and escorted him safely back to his house.

'Words, of course, are the most powerful drug used by humanity,' said Rudyard Kipling famously. The drug turned out to be a lifesaver for Field Marshal Sam Manekshaw (who won for India the Indo-Pakistan War of 1971 that led to the liberation of Bangladesh):

Maneckshaw began his army career in 1932 at the Indian Military Academy, Dehra Dun. Commissioned in the Frontier Force in 1934, he saw action in Burma in the Second World War and displayed exemplary courage.

This brave fighter was so badly wounded during WWII that a British officer, Major General D.T. Cowan, knowing that the Military Cross could not be awarded posthumously, pinned his own Military Cross on Maneckshaw's shirt, believing that the deserving young man would be unable to survive the terrible bullet wounds sustained.

Seeing his precarious condition, the attending Australian surgeon was debating whether it was even worth trying to save Maneckshaw. But then something happened.

> The doctor softly asked Maneckshaw what had happened to him. Even on the verge of death, Maneckshaw jokingly rasped, 'A mule kicked me.'
>
> What convinced the doctor in favour of operating on the seriously wounded soldier? The latter's puckish sense of humour even as he lay dying!

That simple joke, communicated in short gasps, was the single reason why the doctor worked towards saving Maneckshaw's life. Good luck? Yes, but communication made it possible.

Chris Guillebeau, an entrepreneur and blogger, is a world traveller who accomplished the goal of visiting all 193 countries of the world by his 35th birthday. He is also the author of *The $100 Startup*. According to Chris:

> 'I think a lot of fear comes down to three things: fear of failure, fear of success and fear of change, which is especially important. Everyone hates change they can't control. They want other people to change, but from a safe distance.
>
> 'In the writing and entrepreneurial world, I have many fears: fears of judgment, of being misunderstood, of being marginalized, of letting other people down. Each of these can be paralyzing forces if you let them consume you.
>
> 'What I've found really helps me is positive reinforcement. I keep a file of nice things people

have said and that file only exists for me. It's only there for when I want to look at it, and I don't look through it that often, but it's nice to know it's there.

'Even though it's true that negative feedback is more damaging than positive feedback is affirming, as you begin to receive positive feedback, pay attention to it. It helps to ground yourself and get a sense of perspective around the negative feedback you receive.'

Confidence does not come from being right, but from not fearing to be wrong. Remember Wiseman's newspaper experiment? Confident, relaxed persons who were not too worried about the outcome were able to observe the large ad on the second page, whereas those who were anxious and fearful ended up remaining tightly focused on the immediate task and thus missed the magic solution.

The simplest solution comes from Bill Cosby, who said, 'Decide that you want it more than you are afraid of it!' Once that happens, even poor communication can be compensated for. Take the case of Anil Manibhai Naik:

Anil Manibhai Naik, a mechanical engineer, had applied to Larsen & Toubro (L&T) for a job. His chances of success were low. After all, he hadn't graduated from an IIT, but from Birla Vishvakarma College, Gujarat.

His poor English had also resulted in eight mistakes on the very first employment form that he submitted at L&T!

Naik got the job in 1965, but the company reduced their initial monthly salary offer from Rs. 760 to Rs. 670. L&T also offered him a designation lower than initially promised, reportedly because the final interviewer (an Englishman) considered Naik to be arrogant.

Years later, Naik attributed this to the communication gap between him and the Englishman. 'I used to think in Gujarati, then translate it into English; the Englishman perhaps misunderstood what I had intended to say.'

Least cowed down by these setbacks, Naik took the job. Little did he realize then that thirty-eight years later, he would become Chairman of L&T.

In his book *Made in America*, Sam Walton, the founder of Walmart, says that he aspired to become student body president in college, for which the two key qualities needed were confidence and communication:

'I learned early on that one of the secrets to campus leadership was the simplest thing of all: speak to people coming down the sidewalk before they speak to you. I did that in college.

'I did it when I carried my papers. I would always look ahead and speak to the person coming toward me. If I knew them, I would call them by name, but even if I didn't, I would still speak to them.

'Before long, I probably knew more students than anybody in the university, and they recognized me and considered me their friend.'

Communicate more. Communicate better. That's Sam Walton's prescription. Good communication not only helps us respond better to opportunities, it can even create opportunities. The most incredible example is Ronald Reagan, the fortieth president of the United States:

Ronald Reagan had been a radio, film and TV actor before entering politics. Thus, his communication skills were legendary.

In 1987, Reagan stood in front of the Berlin Wall and challenged his Soviet counterpart, saying, 'General Secretary Gorbachev, if you seek peace, if you seek prosperity for the Soviet Union and Eastern Europe, if you seek liberalization, come here to this gate! Mr Gorbachev, open this gate! Mr Gorbachev, tear down this wall!'

The rest, as we know, is history. Twenty-nine months later, the wall came down, governments of Eastern Europe began to collapse and eventually the forces of *perestroika* and *glasnost* (restructuring and transparency) brought the erstwhile Soviet Union tumbling down, creating thousands of new opportunities in politics, business and international relations.

Today, we live in an age of short attention spans. A recent study showed that the average browser in a bookshop spends eight seconds on the front cover and fifteen seconds on the back cover of a book that he/she picks up. Most readers do not get past page eighteen of the average book. How does an author get noticed in such times? Much as we want to believe that books are not judged by their covers, the truth is: they often are. A good cover improves the odds of your book reaching the billing counter. The cover design is the communication of an emotion. Getting it right is vital to clinching the sale. This particular book's cover was designed and redesigned over twenty times.

Similarly, venture capitalists have admitted that the quality of an entrepreneur's pitch has often influenced them to fund the venture.

According to Robert McKee, the world's best known and most respected screenwriting lecturer, a powerful way to persuade people is by '...uniting an idea with an emotion. The best way to do so is by telling a compelling story. In a story, you not only weave a lot of information into the telling, you also arouse your listener's emotions and energy.' The emotion could be conveyed in myriad ways. It could be a casual conversation, postcard, email, facial expression, handshake, book cover, advertisement, video or song:

It was 1963, the year after India had lost the war with China. It had been a terrible defeat for India: 1,383 killed, 1,047 wounded, 1,696 missing and 3,968 soldiers captured as prisoners of war.

Jawaharlal Nehru's naiveté was seen as the key reason for the defeat. Defence minister Krishna Menon had been asked to resign.

In the face of a disunited polity, there was an immediate need for strengthening India's armed forces and instituting reforms within the military. India's permanent foe Pakistan was friendly with China, and it was vital that India stand behind the political leadership with one voice in spite of the defeat. But that was easier said than done. India was a fractured mess at the time.

On January 27, 1963, twenty-four hours after Republic Day, Nehru spoke briefly to a large audience gathered at the Ramlila Maidan, New Delhi.

Then, upon a signal from Nehru, Lata Mangeshkar began singing a song (*Ae Mere Watan Ke Logon*) written by Kavi Pradeep. That song and its singer would become immortal.

After hearing the song, there wasn't a single dry eye in India that day. No one could think of anything other than the martyrs who had sacrificed their lives. If a picture is worth a thousand words, what is a song worth?

Over the next few years, India made substantial investments to upgrade its military hardware and increase the strength of its army, resulting in India winning several later wars with Pakistan. Communication had won the day.

In my first semester as an MBA student at Yale, I was chosen to present a case analysis. I worked on the case the previous day and ran the rather detailed (and lengthy) Power Point presentation by my team members. One of my team members, who had worked in advertising, said, 'A speech should be like a woman's skirt: long enough to cover the subject matter but short enough to hold the audience's attention.' I spent the rest of the night reworking the presentation to half its original length. Many years later, after I had finished writing my first novel, my editor reminded me of the words of Hawthorne: 'Easy reading is damn hard writing.' You bet it is!

I end this section with a short poignant story to emphasize the importance of communication in trapping opportunities:

A blind beggar sat at a street corner with a cardboard sign next to his empty tin cup: 'I am blind. Please help.'

A young writer passing by observed that people were completely unmoved. No one was dropping any alms.

The writer flipped the blind man's cardboard sign and wrote a new message. Almost magically people began putting money into the cup. Soon the cup was overflowing.

Simply amazed, the blind man asked a stranger to read out the new message to him.

The new message read: 'It's a beautiful day. You can see it. I cannot.'

What does this story tell us? Simply that there were enough moneyed people passing by—opportunities. A simple change in communication strategy had found a way of harnessing those opportunities.

9		**INFORMATION**	Raise	✓
Attitude		***Lucky people stay informed and absorb new ideas***	Recognize	✓
Approach	✓		Respond	✓

The power of information is often undervalued. Simply staying informed increases the chances of opportunities coming to our attention. The value of information is best illustrated by a story from Dhirubhai Ambani's life:

It is well-known that Dhirubhai gathered information from any and every source—

information about governments, policies, products, competitors, employees, politics and a lot more.

A candidate attended a personal interview with Dhirubhai for a senior position in Reliance, but he had other offers too. Reliance was not his first choice.

At the interview, Dhirubhai casually asked: 'How is your father's health?'

Apparently, the young man's father, a senior professor and research scholar, had undergone a bypass surgery following a heart attack a few days ago.

Dhirubhai's information network had already briefed him of the developments, much to the candidate's surprise.

Need I say that the candidate took the Reliance offer? Information had met opportunity.

Consider yet another, much older, example from India's business history:

In 1861, the US Civil War broke out. Until then, the cotton mills of England sourced only twenty per cent of their raw material requirements from India, with their major supply coming from America. As a result of the war, the demand for Indian cotton shot through the roof.

The greatest cotton speculator of the times was Premchand Roychand. During that age when no telegraph line existed between India and Europe, the imperfect information flow created a terrific opportunity. Mind you, the opportunity was available to all, but it was only Roychand who was able to exploit it so very effectively.

In those days, local cotton prices in Mumbai would change to reflect international prices only after English ships docked and sailors came ashore with the latest price information.

Roychand would send his agents out on boats to meet the English ships coming to Mumbai. Their primary task? To learn and convey to him the latest London cotton prices *before* the ships docked at port.

Roychand's advance team gave him a head start over all the other cotton traders of Mumbai. Duly armed with this advance information, Roychand would take massive positions in the market before anyone else knew where prices were headed. Obviously, Roychand reaped enormous profits from the cotton boom.

Good luck? Yes, but it emerged from remaining informed.

Being aware of what is happening around us, listening to informed individuals, keeping track of the news and reading books is a crucial part of the opportunity flow. Take the case of Jamsetji Tata. In Jamsetji's biography, author R.M. Lala says:

Jamsetji was among the early Indians to benefit from a Western education. He chose the field of business as a career, but it did not run his whole life.

'For though Mr Tata was a businessman, he was also a scholar… Learning was, indeed, his chief recreation and delight,' wrote F.R. Harris.

He knew the value of reading and of creative thinking that springs up when a mind is at leisure with itself. Throughout his life he kept time each day for reading and contemplation. In these couple of hours of quiet—before he went to office (about 1:00 pm) and usually after dinner—his great schemes were conceived.

On the other hand, Mohandas Gandhi (later to be known as Mahatma Gandhi) was not a voracious reader. However, whatever he read seemed to affect him rather deeply. In one particular instance, it changed him dramatically. The book in question was John Ruskin's *Unto This Last: Four Essays on the First Principles of Political Economy*.

In 1903, when Gandhi, aged thirty-four years, was leaving for Durban, his friend Henry Polak saw him off at Johannesburg railway station and gave him Ruskin's book for the journey.

Gandhi read the book from cover to cover during the twenty-four hour train journey, and the Gandhi who stepped off the train at Durban was a transformed man. Gandhi had decided to change his entire life to match the ideals prescribed by John Ruskin.

Many years later, examining what he owed to Great Britain, Gandhi wrote, 'Great Britain gave me Ruskin, whose *Unto This Last* … transformed me overnight from a lawyer and city-dweller into a rustic, living away from Durban on a farm, three miles from the nearest railway station!'

Had he not read Ruskin, Gandhi would have probably remained a lawyer and the great transformation from Mohandas to Mahatma would never have happened!

The profound change that a single book could bring in Gandhi's life shows how new ideas can open up new vistas of thinking. And more often than not, opportunities present themselves in the form of ideas. One may not be able to act immediately on the idea, but that does not make it any less powerful:

Hasmukhbhai Parekh lived in a chawl with his father. He somehow managed to study, work part-time and then, incredibly, earn a degree from the London School of Economics. His stint as a lecturer at St. Xavier's College, Mumbai for three years transformed him into an excellent speaker.

After working with a stockbroking firm for some years, he joined ICICI, one of the earliest financial institutions sponsored by the World Bank in cooperation with India and America. Joining ICICI as Deputy General Manager in 1956, he retired as its Chairman in 1978.

At age sixty-eight, most men look back on their years and prepare for a life of retirement, but not Hasmukhbhai. He dropped in to meet the-then Secretary of Finance, Dr Manmohan Singh, and sought his cooperation for establishing a new company. It was to be called the Housing Development Finance Corporation (or HDFC).

Some years later, Hasmukhbhai's friend and prolific writer R.M. Lala asked what had inspired him to establish HDFC. Hasmukhbhai replied, 'I thought of it when I was in England at the London School of Economics.'

'But that must have been almost forty years ago!' exclaimed Lala.

Hasmukhbhai nodded. Seeing how people bought their houses on mortgage in England, he always wanted Indians also to avail the same facility. After harbouring the idea for forty years, he acted on it by launching HDFC immediately upon retirement from ICICI.

HDFC would eventually become a \$3.44 billion behemoth under the stewardship of Hasmukhbhai's nephew Deepak Parekh.

Just look at the story of Howard Schultz, Chairman and CEO of Starbucks, who picked up his greatest idea and business opportunity from a routine business trip to Italy:

The brand Starbucks is synonymous with coffee. Howard Schultz held several jobs before becoming manager at Hammarplast, a Swedish coffee machine manufacturer. In his book *Pour Your Heart Into It*, he wrote:

'In 1981, while working for Hammarplast, I noticed a strange phenomenon. A little retailer in Seattle was placing unusually large orders for a certain type of drip coffeemaker, a simple plastic cone set on a thermos. I investigated. Starbucks Coffee, Tea and Spice had only four small stores then, yet it was buying this product in quantities larger than Macy's.'

Schultz visited Starbucks and realized that they were quality retailers of premium coffee. Some months later, Schultz joined Starbucks as their Director (Marketing).

Shortly thereafter, while visiting Italy, Schultz saw coffee shops on almost every street corner. He observed that the coffee shops served not only as transaction points, but also as informal meeting places.

On returning to the US, Schultz presented this idea to the original Starbucks owners. Being coffee retailers, not restaurant owners, they rejected his proposal.

But Schultz's idea from Italy refused to die. He eventually left Starbucks to start his own coffee chain, Il Giornale.

Two years later, he bought the rights to the Starbucks brand for $3 million and renamed his flourishing chain of coffee shops.

The story of Walchand Hirachand Doshi given in Gita Piramal's *Business Legends* is a perfect example of how idea absorption influences luck. The first paragraph is about Doshi 'flitting from idea to idea'; the next reveals what he was actually able to achieve during his lifetime:

And as Walchand flitted from idea to idea, semi-implemented proposals piled up like old newspapers. A visit to Hollywood enthused him so much that he wanted to set up a film studio. He invited V. Shantharam to join him, but the idea never took off. He bought a mining lease, which brought him little more than bills. He acquired a foundry, which he couldn't manage profitably. He built a saw mill, which had to be closed down.

Apart from his achievements in shipping, Walchand built several of India's enduring monuments. His construction firm built the Bhor Ghats tunnel (through which trains shuttle between Mumbai and Pune). He laid the huge pipes, which bring water to Mumbai from Tansa lake, and numerous bridges, dams and railway tracks all over the country. Walchand also built India's first shipyard, India's first aircraft factory and India's first car plant.

Lucky people notice things. They hang on to ideas. They absorb stuff. They're curious about things that catch their attention.

Times have changed. Ideas reach us not only through books but also through various other channels: discussions, social media, the web, TV, even movies. The channel is unimportant, but staying informed and absorbing ideas seems to be one of the key traits of lucky people.

10		**GOODNESS**	Raise	✓
Attitude	✓	***Lucky people understand the power of goodness***	Recognize	
Approach			Respond	✓

There are some meetings and encounters that one simply never forgets:

As a college student, I spent my afternoons working in my father's office. One day, my father told me an important visitor would be dropping in at our office. It was Mr J.R.D. Tata.

After spending a few minutes enquiring about the products that he was interested in, JRD had tea with my father. In between, several of my father's staff members dropped in to request Mr Tata for photographs and autographs.

JRD did not refuse a single request. In fact, he suggested that a group photograph be taken so that staff members who had been left out could also be included. Not once did he indicate that he was in a hurry to leave, or that he had more important meetings lined up, even though his worried secretary kept checking her watch.

He shook hands with everyone, asking them their names and their respective roles in office. He even asked whether they were happy working for my dad's company! It was almost like a father figure ensuring that all members of the flock were happy!

I learned something rather important that day: It's nice to be important but it's more important to be nice.

I would later read that Mr Tata had once said, 'To be a leader, you have got to lead human beings with affection.' It was simply impossible not to like him. Probably that was the reason people found it hard to refuse his requests. Possibly that was also why he was so lucky. His inherent niceness attracted opportunities, while also making it easier for him to find and retain people who could act on the opportunities that came his way.

Observe successful people and you will find that all of them have understood the power of goodness. This anecdote from Abraham Lincoln's life also illustrates it:

In his legal practice, Abraham Lincoln discouraged unnecessary litigation. Nor was Lincoln greedy.

When requested to sue an impoverished debtor for $2.50, Lincoln tried his best to discourage the client from pursuing the debt, but the man was determined and wanted revenge.

When Lincoln saw that the creditor was unlikely to be dissuaded, he asked for and received a rather substantial legal fee of $10.

He gave half of this to the defendant, who willingly confessed to the debt and paid the $2.50 that he owed, thus settling the matter to the entire satisfaction of Lincoln's client!

Lucky individuals are not only nice—polite, humble and considerate—but are also intuitively aware of the power of karma. They understand that the greater the positive deeds they put out in the universe, the better the chances of their attracting good luck.

My friend Alok Kejriwal, CEO and co-founder of Games2Win, recounts that when he was sixteen, he helped his grandfather to supply potable water to the ONGC rigs off Mumbai High.

On one occasion, while the tanker was being unloaded, Alok casually addressed the ONGC inspector as 'yaar' (Hindi equivalent of chum or buddy).

The inspector felt insulted that a kid could be so 'familiar' with him, and blew a fuse. As a result, the ONGC business dwindled.

Alok's mother arranged for him to meet Shashi Ruia, chairman of Essar. Essar had substantial dealings with ONGC and a word from the company could possibly soothe ruffled feathers.

Shashi Ruia heard Alok's story, picked up his phone and spoke to the concerned inspector in a jovial way. Within a few hours, it was business as usual for Alok.

Twenty-six years later, Alok fondly reported in his blog how 'Shashi Uncle' had helped him even though he probably had far more important and pressing matters to deal with.

Unfortunately, the phrase 'being nice' has received a nasty rap on many fronts. You must have heard the phrase 'nice guys finish last'. As for 'nice girls', they never seem to have any fun as per popular opinion! Our world has succeeded in convincing us that being nice is unappealing.

Scientifically though, it is a proven fact that being nice results in increased dopamine levels, which provide a natural 'high'. These happy hormones make us much more positive and enable us to look at new opportunities with the right attitude. In effect, being nice not only makes others happy, it also makes us happy. And being happy and positive about life is a key factor in attracting luck.

During Anna Hazare's agitation for the Lok Pal bill, Aamir Khan decided to throw his weight behind the activist. Reminiscing about his interaction, Aamir said, 'When I met Anna, he told me "Happiness is the only thing that when you give it, you get it in return." And those words touched me and I strongly believe in it.'

It is fashionable these days to advise 'be yourself' as the solution to life. Actress Judy Garland suggested, 'Always be a first-rate version of yourself, instead of a second-rate version of somebody else.' The problem is that 'being yourself' is often not enough. American journalist Mignon McLaughlin rightly observed, 'Don't be yourself. Be someone a little nicer!'

An apt example is a casual visitor's narration of an incident at Mumbai airport's domestic arrival terminal:

Late one night, a group of top executives poured out of the arrival lounge. Most ordered their chauffeurs to pick their baggage and shouted at them for perceived delays. But one tall gentleman smilingly said: 'You are not paid to carry my luggage but to drive me home; please get the car.' He tugged his entire luggage to his car by himself.

After a while, when I realized that the tall man was none other than Ratan Tata, I involuntarily raised my hand to salute him. At the same time, I wondered about others who did not try to emulate his humility in spite of moving with him.

In our daily interactions with people, it costs absolutely nothing to smile. How hard is it to acknowledge the presence of someone by using his or her name? Is it really that difficult to express gratitude for a favour received? The American poet Maya Angelou astutely observed, 'People will forget what you said, people will forget what you did, but will never forget how you made them feel.'

While *The Secret* tells us that positive thoughts bring positive changes in our lives, we should remember that positive deeds also have a karmic effect:

When Mohandas Gandhi once boarded a train, one of his sandals slipped off and landed on the track. He was unable to retrieve it because the train had begun moving.

To the surprise of his companions, Gandhi removed his other sandal and carefully threw it back so that it landed close to the first.

When another passenger asked him why, Gandhi smilingly replied. 'The poor man who finds the footwear lying on the track will now have a pair that he can use.'

Often, niceness is not about what you do, but what you don't. In fact, there is an old proverb: 'The kindest word in the world is the unkind word left unsaid.' Two examples stand out in this regard:

Asked which orchestra gave him the most pleasure to conduct, Zubin Mehta tactfully refused to single out any particular favourite, saying, 'What would a devout Muslim answer as to which of his wives he preferred?'

When a newspaper (to which he subscribed) mistakenly published an announcement of his death, Rudyard Kipling immediately wrote to the editor, 'I've just read that I'm dead. Don't forget to delete me from your list of subscribers.'

By not explicitly stating the name of his favourite orchestra, Mehta was ensuring that all the orchestras that he worked with would remain motivated to perform their best. Similarly, by making a joke out of a mistaken obituary, Kipling was avoiding unnecessary recriminations.

Harvard University psychologist William James summed it up beautifully. 'The art of being wise is the art of knowing what to overlook.' This often requires us to consciously steer away from negative thoughts or discussions. Consider this:

In ancient Greece, Socrates was known to place a premium on knowledge. When an acquaintance visited the philosopher and began, 'Do you know what I just heard about your friend?'

'Just wait for a moment,' interrupted Socrates. 'Before telling me anything more, I'd like you to pass a little test. It's called the Triple Filter Test.'

'Triple filter?' asked the acquaintance.

'That's right,' said Socrates. 'Before you tell me something about my friend, I wish to filter what you are about to say. The first filter is Truth. Have you ensured that what you are about to tell me is absolutely true?'

'No,' replied the acquaintance. 'I just heard about it and wanted to share it with you ...'

'Fine,' said Socrates. 'So you cannot be sure whether the information is true or false. Let's try the second filter, the filter of Goodness. Are you about to tell me something about my friend that is good?'

'No, actually ...'

'So you want to share something that is bad about him. But you are not certain that it's true. You may still pass the test because there is a third filter: the filter of Usefulness. Is what you wish to convey going to be useful to me?'

'No, I don't think so ...' began the acquaintance.

'Well,' demanded Socrates, 'if what you want

to tell me is neither true nor good nor even useful, why tell it to me at all?'

Probably the Socrates story has inspired the Rotarians' four-way test. One: is it the truth? Two: is it fair to all concerned? Three: will it build goodwill and better friendships? Four: will it be beneficial to all concerned?

Hundreds of small actions add up to niceness. Returning a phone call; behaving courteously with one's colleagues and subordinates; remembering a birthday; praising a subordinate's effort, overlooking minor deficiencies... The list is rather long. Sometimes it simply involves doing what is 'right' rather than what is 'required'. Consider this incident from Rajinikanth's life:

Rajinikanth is probably the most enduring actor and cultural icon of India. Born and raised in poverty, he began acting in theatre while working in the Bangalore Metropolitan Transport Corporation as a bus conductor. The bus conductor to film idol story is the stuff of legends.

What is often forgotten is that in 2002, Rajinikanth starred in *Baba*, and had also written its screenplay. Though released with great media hype, box office collections were short of the high bids paid by distributors. As a result, many distributors incurred huge losses.

Rajinikanth personally repaid the losses incurred by most of the distributors even though he was not legally obligated to.

Five years later, his next movie *Chandramukhi* was released. A smashing success, it set the record of being the longest running Tamil film. Why? Because of the immense support that Rajinikanth enjoyed from the distributor community.

Being nice also tends to be a wise investment. For example, Abraham Lincoln selflessly withdrew from a Senate race in the 1830s, but ended up winning the endorsement of his rival in the next election.

Venture capitalist David Hornik, whose generosity with competitors is legendary, has always had the very best access to start-ups as a result of favours that he dispensed. Thus, there is a clear correlation between being nice and favourable future opportunities. Take another example, one from the world of advertising:

Linda Kaplan Thaler, chairman of ad agency Publicis Kaplan Thaler and co-author of *The Power of Nice: How to Conquer the Business World With Kindness*, wrote, 'I grew up in the Bronx and I've heard a lot of four-letter words and none of them are as powerful as N-I-C-E.'

In 1999, her agency was approached by a large insurance company to pitch for an ad campaign. When Thaler asked how they had heard of her, she was pleasantly surprised to learn that two people to whom she had been kind in the past had recommended her.

'Many people don't recognize that so much business can be generated from positive deeds and actions,' said Thaler.

The bottom line? Niceness increases the probability that opportunities would be thrown your way by your network. Being nice not only results in positive word of mouth; it also ensures that someone else's door remains open for you in future. And doesn't one need an open door for good luck to walk in?

One particular story from Winston Churchill's life is a perfect example of the power of goodness:

In the summer of 1941, Sergeant James Allen Ward was awarded the Victoria Cross for climbing out onto the wing of his Wellington bomber, 13,000 feet above earth, to extinguish a fire in the starboard engine. Secured only by a rope around his waist, he managed to not only smother the fire but also to return along the wing to the aircraft's cabin.

Churchill, an admirer as well as a performer of daring exploits, summoned the shy New Zealander to 10, Downing Street.

Ward, dumbstruck with awe in the presence of Churchill, found himself incapable of answering the PM's questions. Churchill observed the floundering hero with sympathy.

'You must feel very humble and awkward in my presence,' said Churchill.

'Yes, sir,' replied Ward hesitantly.

'Then you can imagine how humble and awkward I feel in yours,' Churchill responded.

I cannot imagine a modern-day politician showing that sort of humility to an officer of the armed forces. It was these little gestures that made Churchill a hero among his people and enabled him to defeat Germany against all odds. Humility is also one of the key reasons why some people are able to cultivate relationships better than others.

Thomas Carlyle rightly said, 'A great man shows his greatness by the way he treats little men.' Nearer home, Shirdi Sai Baba said, 'If you are wealthy, be humble. Plants bend when they bear fruit.'

Keeping one's ego in check and having one's feet firmly planted on the ground are fundamental requirements for opportunity to flow. If one has a bloated opinion of oneself, how would one be open to listening to others or accepting the ideas they may have? According to A.H.Z. Carr, author of *How to Attract Good Luck*:

'Probably no human frailty is more likely to bring bad luck than an exaggerated need for appreciation.

This unhappy state of mind, which usually grows out of a rooted feeling of insecurity, drives its victim to advertise his importance and demand that the busy world pay attention to him. Inevitably, he cuts off favourable chances, which might otherwise emanate from others. Because the egoist tends to be inattentive when others are talking, he causes acquaintances to take a passive attitude in conversation and to withhold information and ideas that might have had luck value for him.'

An inflated ego often prevents us from asking questions that we believe 'sound stupid'. The problem is that not asking those questions means that we are shutting out potential opportunities. Management guru Tom Peters says, 'Ask dumb questions: How come all computer commands come from keyboards? Somebody asked that one first. Hence, the mouse!'

The old adage 'What goes around comes around' is based on a deeper karmic theory that the more one gives, the more one gets. One should never discount the value of karma. An incident from the University of Wisconsin illustrates this beautifully:

Many years ago at the University of Wisconsin there was a group of literary men, all extremely creative in their use of the English language: would-be poets, novelists and dramatists. Meeting each week to read and ruthlessly critique each other's works, they called themselves the Stranglers.

As a reaction, a group of upcoming women writers also started a club at Wisconsin. Deciding to call themselves the Wranglers, they too met regularly to read and critique each other's work, but they tended to encourage and praise rather than criticize.

Two decades later, when an alumnus carried out a study of his classmates' careers, he observed a significant difference between the careers of the Stranglers vis-à-vis the Wranglers. Not a single Strangler had been able to attain stature in the literary world, while the Wranglers had produced more than six women writers of national and international renown.

What does that tell us? First, that there is value in positive reinforcement and in being nice. But more importantly, if we can't find something good in other people's work, how can we expect others to find something good in ours? Generosity in spirit and actions is a key element in furthering opportunities. Here are a few examples:

Sir Jamsetjee Jeejeebhoy, the first Indian Baronet and Bombay's wealthiest man in the nineteenth century, started his career by selling bottles. He used the immense wealth that he created to establish hospitals and to found the JJ School of Arts. Legends of the time say that when Sir Jeejeebhoy drove around the city in his two-horse carriage, he would sit between two bags of coins from which he would distribute money to beggars lining his route.

In 2013, Azim Premji became the first Indian to sign up for the Giving Pledge, an undertaking by charitable billionaires to contribute a major chunk of their wealth to philanthropic causes. When he signed the pledge, he had already committed nine thousand crores to the cause of education.

Warren Buffett, the world's fourth-richest man, will give away ninety-nine per cent of his wealth during his lifetime, and Gates, the second-wealthiest man on the planet, will donate at least half his riches to fulfil their pledges.

Bollywood superstar Salman Khan is best known for delivering a series of hundred-crore blockbuster films. But what is often forgotten is that his apparel brand 'Being Human' records annual sales of Rs. 179 crores. The royalties received on this amount go to support the education and healthcare initiatives of Salman's charitable venture, The Salman Khan Foundation.

Why bother to make money only to give it away? There is an old Chinese proverb: 'A bit of fragrance always clings to the hand that gives roses.' Most of us are not billionaires, but that should not prevent us from doing something good for others.

Many years ago when I was struggling to find a publisher, a professor from my alma mater requested my help in writing a speech for him. Though it required a substantial investment of time, I acceded to his request to his great satisfaction. He was very pleased with the result.

A few months later, when my novel began appearing in bookstores, he asked me how sales were doing. I replied that I was happy with sales, but was facing an uphill task regarding publicity. My professor immediately sent me his friend's phone number. 'Give him a call,' he said. 'I'm quite sure he will be able to help you.'

I later learnt that his friend was editor of a national newspaper. A couple of weeks later, my first major newspaper interview happened.

Good luck? Sure. But some investment of prior effort made it happen.

There is one caveat though. Giving with the intention of receiving back negates its very purpose. Motivational speaker Brian Tracy reminds us, 'Always give without remembering and always receive without forgetting.'

And then, leave Lady Luck to take her own majestic course!

11		PASSION	Raise	
Attitude	✓	***Lucky people seek ways to get paid for their passion***	Recognize	✓
Approach	✓		Respond	✓

Prior to my writing avatar, the only thing I had ever trained for was the world of business:

When I was twelve, my father would send me during my summer vacations to learn bookkeeping from our family accountant. Passionate about reading from an early age, I was always to be found carrying a different book every week, sent to me by my maternal grand-uncle, a poet and writer.

When our accountant observed several errors I had made while tallying the trial balance, he admonished me, 'If you gave a little more time to bookkeeping rather than book reading, there wouldn't be so many errors in your work!'

I protested. I argued that reading books was my passion. Smiling wryly, the old man declared, 'If you must indulge your passion then try reading a balance sheet! At least you would be doing something worthwhile.'

Some weeks later, I spoke with my grand uncle about this exchange of words.

The old man thought about it for a minute and said, 'Lakshmi (wealth) without Saraswati (knowledge) is always a problem. Ganesh, the ultimate symbol of good luck, is always shown seated between Lakshmi and Saraswati. The presence of *both* is vital for good luck to happen.'

He paused for thought.

'The truth is that the only thing that money gives you is the freedom of not having to worry about money. More than balancing the figures, try balancing Lakshmi and Saraswati in your life.'

That particular lesson has stayed with me till today. British author and scholar Robert Graves famously quipped, 'There is no money in poetry but then, there's no poetry in money either.' The tug-of-war between money and poetry—sustenance and passion—would continue to remain an integral part of my life.

Please don't think that I'm discounting the value of money. One needs money to live in reasonable comfort; to be secure from life's vagaries; to be in a position to enjoy simple pleasures like a meal out with the family, a short holiday or a movie. But beyond that, for many people, money is simply a proxy for success. Money enables them to 'keep score'.

Dhirubhai Ambani, the founder of Reliance Industries and India's definitive rags-to-riches icon, is believed to have said, 'Does making money excite me? No, but I have to make money for my shareholders. What excites me is achievement, doing something difficult.'

We also find that money was never the sole motivator for some of the most successful individuals:

P.V. Narasimha Rao, India's ninth Prime Minister, oversaw major economic transformation and was personally responsible for dismantling India's 'Licence Raj'. He is often referred to as the 'Father of Indian Economic Reforms' for steering tough economic and political legislation through Parliament even though he headed a minority government.

Funnily enough, this visionary who saved India from financial ruin was invariably in personal financial distress. One of his sons had to be educated with the financial assistance of Rao's son-in-law. Rao even had difficulty in paying tuition for a daughter who was studying Medicine.

It is said that Rao ordered the sale of his house at Banjara Hills (in Hyderabad) in order to clear his advocates' fees. Apparently Rao was afraid of dying before clearing these debts.

Looking back at my own life, I realize: Had I been running solely after money, I would never have sat down to write my first book. I would have outright discarded the option of pursuing a creative endeavour, considering the meagre remuneration that writers usually get.

Look at another example:

One of the biggest cash generating machines in the world is the search engine company Google. At last count, it earned $7,129,629 per hour—or around fifteen billion dollars per quarter. It is now difficult to recall that Google began in 1996 as a mere research project by Larry Page and Sergey Brin while they were PhD students at Stanford.

We are now accustomed to seeing search-driven ads on Google and it is easy to forget that the company had no advertisements until 2000. There was simply no revenue for the first five years of its existence, no business model at all!

The founders were single-mindedly focused on simply building the world's best search engine. Money was seen as a by-product. Could that attitude possibly explain Google's phenomenal good fortune?

Henry Ford reportedly held the view: 'A business that makes nothing but money is a poor business.' The view crystallizing in my head was that one needs money to live comfortably, but beyond a point, it becomes less relevant. Wasn't it possible that our mad quest for gold might render us incapable of seeing the silver lining? Could we possibly be missing opportunities by limiting our field of vision by wearing money blinkers?

My dilemma was finally solved during a flight:

On a flight from Mumbai to New York, an artist was seated next to me.

Explaining that he sold his paintings to large hotels chains and multinational companies, he said, 'All of them need art for the walls of their guest rooms, executive cabins and public spaces. I am happy to execute it for them at a reasonable price.'

I found his business fascinating. I had always believed that artists were wandering souls with very little business sense. He laughed.

'The best way to live your life? Find a way to get paid for your passion,' he said. 'That's precisely what I have done.'

His words reminded me of the famous artist M.F. Husain, who painted cinema posters in Mumbai early in his career in order to survive as an artist.

Picasso, the world's most famous painter, was reportedly asked if it tired him to stand in front of a canvas for three or four hours while painting. 'No,' he replied. 'That's why painters live so long. While I work, I leave my body outside the door, the way Muslims take off their shoes before entering the mosque.' Passion makes one forget that it's work.

Richard Branson, the founder of Virgin, says:

'Almost all our new ventures come about from our thinking up a product or service that we believe people really want. You'll notice that making a profit hasn't entered the picture yet. It's rare—for me or for the team—to consider only the money that can be made. I feel it's pointless to approach investing with the question, "How can I make lots of money?" When it's time to decide whether or not to go ahead, the decision must come from your heart. If you pursue your passions, your ideas will be more likely to succeed.'

In effect, if an opportunity coincides with one's passion, the odds of making it remunerative are significantly higher. This is because one's desire to succeed at one's passion is far greater than one's desire to succeed at anything else. This little story about Greek philosopher Socrates explains what I mean:

When a young man visited Socrates in search of wisdom, he was surprised when Socrates took him to a lake and dunked his head under water.

As the man struggled to come up for air, Socrates continued holding him under.

Later, after recovering, when the young man asked Socrates why he had nearly drowned him, Socrates replied, 'What was it that you most wanted when you were under water?'

'Air,' the young man replied.

Socrates responded, 'When your desire for wisdom is as great as your desire to breathe, you will find wisdom.'

Passion is like the need for air. When one is passionate about something, one will do everything possible to make it happen. Confucius astutely observed, 'Choose a job you love, and you will never have to work a day in your life.'

The Socrates story is seen repeated in the life of Lakshmi Mittal, chairman and CEO of ArcelorMittal, the world's largest steel manufacturing company:

Towards the end of 2005, Aditya Mittal, son of steel magnate Lakshmi Mittal, met Alain Davezac, Arcelor's senior vice president of international business development, to discuss ways by which the two companies could collaborate.

It was decided that their bosses, Guy Dolle and Lakshmi Mittal, should meet. A dinner was organized and the topic of merging Mittal Steel with Arcelor was discussed only briefly. Guy Dolle, CEO of Arcelor, dismissed the idea given the different company cultures.

Dolle thought the matter had ended there, but was reportedly shocked when Lakshmi Mittal telephoned him just thirteen days later. The purpose of Mittal's call was to inform Dolle that Mittal was announcing a hostile takeover bid for Arcelor.

A surprised Alain Davezac immediately phoned friends in India to find out what had prompted Mittal's actions. They answered, 'Just see where he comes from. He has the kind of hunger you Europeans will never understand.'

12		UNLEARN	Raise	✓
Attitude	✓	***Lucky people unlearn old attitudes and approaches***	Recognize	✓
Approach			Respond	✓

John Grisham had to forget he was a lawyer in order to write *A Time To Kill*. Dan Brown had to forget he was an academic when he sat down to write the *Da Vinci Code*. I had to forget I was a businessman to write *The Rozabal Line*, *Chanakya's Chant* and *The Krishna Key*.

In an effort to forget—or unlearn—my business avatar, I even discarded my name Ashwin Sanghi and wrote my first novel under the pseudonym Shawn Haigins (an anagram of my name). I was worried that some of my writings (including the mildly erotic passages) might scandalize the business community that I dealt with! I was also worried that my writing might be inhibited by such considerations if I used my own name.

These examples led to my next insight into the theoretical framework for my luck harvesting system. It is best illustrated through an oft-repeated story:

In Japan, during the Meiji era, there lived a great Zen master Nan-in. One day, a respected university professor visited him to inquire about Zen philosophy.

As the host, Nan-in poured tea into a cup for the professor from a kettle. He filled his visitor's cup but continued pouring.

The professor watched the tea overflowing from the cup until he could no longer restrain himself. 'Stop! It's spilling out. No more tea will go into that cup!'

Nan-in smiled.

'The cup has a limited capacity,' said Nan-in. 'You are like the cup. You are full of opinions, beliefs, prejudices and attitudes. How can I possibly show you Zen unless you are willing to empty your cup?'

The point being made was this: one needs to be willing to unlearn in order to learn. One needs to unclutter in order to be capable of receiving from the cosmic.

For many people, the concept of unlearning makes no sense, possibly because they see it as letting go of knowledge. This is a fallacy. Unlearning is about letting go of negative behaviour patterns that create a bad attitude. After all, attitude is a key factor in determining one's response to opportunities.

Some examples of bad attitudes affecting people in everyday situations:

Job seeker: 'This interview is a sham. They have already decided whom to hire. No point in wasting my time.'

Investor: 'I have seen such offers before. There is no value to investing in companies in this sector.'

Musician: 'I have performed here hundreds of times. I can afford to go on stage without a sound check or rehearsal.'

The job seeker's past prevents him from increasing the number of opportunities that come his way. The investor's past prevents him from recognizing new opportunities. The musician's past prevents him from responding to recognized opportunities, thus reducing chances of a successful outcome.

What is the solution? Maybe this seemingly minor incident from my life offers a solution:

A year ago, my wife decided to have our living room walls repainted. While we were leaving for a week's holiday in Goa, she asked the painters to complete the job in our absence.

Upon our return, we were surprised to find the job unfinished. The painters had started applying a fresh coat of paint on the very morning of our return. Obviously, the living room was still a mess.

Rather irritated about having our living room out of bounds, my wife asked the painters the reason for the delay.

The supervisor replied that old paint had accumulated on our walls over several years. 'How can I get new paint to stick if I don't get rid of the old paint first? Stripping off old paint and plaster is seventy per cent of the job. Repainting is only thirty per cent!'

It seems like common sense, right? One can't expect to apply fresh paint without stripping off the older layers. This principle applies to almost everything that we do.

Kishore Biyani, CEO of Future Group and India's retail king, once said in an interview:

'Most people are trained to be preservers. It is great to be a preserver. But for us, whoever has to create has to destroy. Without destroying, you cannot create anything new. That is also the law of nature. Look at the seasons. Everything gets destroyed to create something new. But unfortunately, business does not take any cues from nature. None of the business schools take anything from nature. One cannot go against the flow of nature. In our group, we don't follow business principles. We follow the principles of nature.'

What does one mean by unlearning? It is simply ridding oneself of preconditioning. An example from the world of television demonstrates how one can leverage the absence of preconditioning to enhance one's luck:

In 1990, he was watching reports of the Gulf War on CNN. While others wondered how and when the war would end, he wondered why India did not have a private satellite channel like CNN.

Through a common friend, he quickly arranged a meeting with Doordarshan's chief engineer, who revealed that the laws did not permit broadcasting by the private sector.

He toyed with the idea of setting up a channel in Nepal that would beam terrestrially into India, but soon realized that it would be impossible for the signals from Nepal to reach several Indian cities.

He then examined the idea of video vans that would tour the country allowing villagers to watch movies, but decided that ad revenues would be insufficient to support the venture.

He soon heard about Asiasat, a satellite that could broadcast into India. He followed up with Asiasat's CEO, only to be told that the transponders had been entirely leased to Satellite Television of the Asian Region (more commonly known as STAR).

After trying for many months, he finally got an appointment with Richard Li, son of Li Ka Shing (the owner of STAR), but his offer of $5 million was rejected.

STAR then went scouting for other Indian companies who would be interested in their services, but no one was able to match the $5 million offer. STAR was forced to accept his offer.

Funnily enough, the man who had made the $5 million bid did not even possess the cash at the time. Subhash Chandra would raise the capital for Zee TV much later from a Hong Kong-based fund.

'The existing media companies felt that satellite TV would not succeed in India. Since I did not know anything about the media business, I had nothing to fear,' Subhash Chandra revealed many years later.

In effect, had he had been *conditioned* by the broadcasting industry, Chandra would never have bid $5 million. His lack of conditioning allowed him to bid aggressively.

Henry Ford summed up the issue of negative conditioning by saying, 'I am looking for a lot of men who have an infinite capacity to *not* know what *can't* be done!' Henry Ford would know. Going bankrupt at age forty, he still went on to create the world's automobile industry!

The value of no preconditioning can be illustrated by an example from my own life:

After writing each novel, I would spend days poring over my editor's suggestions.

One day, while discussing my latest work, she said that she loved reading my material because it was completely different from anything else that came before her.

'Maybe it's because I have no goddamned idea of what I'm doing,' I joked. The truth is that I had always felt that my lack of training in creative writing and literature was a liability. I was almost ashamed of my deficiencies.

She didn't reply immediately, but sent me an email a couple of hours later. She had reproduced a quote of Somerset Maugham, the English dramatist and novelist: 'There are three rules for writing the novel. Unfortunately no one knows what they are.'

An absence of preconditioning and training is often a big advantage, because it allows you to remain fresh and innovative. Unlearning is simply the ability to rid oneself of preconditioning.

Gautam Mukunda, a professor at the Harvard Business School, studied several political, business, and military leaders, and classified them in two groups: *filtered leaders*, insiders whose careers followed the usual progression of their sector; and *unfiltered leaders*, who were either outsiders with virtually no experience of the sector or had got their jobs through odd chance. Do you know who the most effective leaders were? You guessed right. The unfiltered lot!

Einstein went to the extent of saying that the only thing that had interfered with his learning was his education! Lack of conditioning—in this case education—makes one much more receptive to a new, untried or untested idea. The number of successful people who dropped out of school or college is pretty impressive: Thomas Edison, Benjamin Franklin, Dhirubhai Ambani, Bill Gates, Richard Branson, John D. Rockefeller, Walt Disney, Charles Dickens… the list is pretty long.

I am certainly not suggesting that one should drop out of school to improve the odds of one's success! Education often provides one with a network of friends and alumni that can increase the opportunities that come your way. It also helps get the proverbial foot-in-the-door when it comes to recruitment opportunities.

But while the network helps increase potential opportunities, the conditioning created by education often seems to prevent us from recognizing opportunities. Our school and university systems seem to encourage a uniform way of thinking. Being able to think outside the framework of one's education and training seems to be a key factor in attracting luck.

13		LEVERAGE	Raise	✓
Attitude		***Lucky people leverage preparation, planning and potential***	Recognize	✓
Approach	✓		Respond	✓

The Roman philosopher Seneca observed, 'Luck is what happens when preparation meets opportunity.'

Sometimes we are inadequately prepared for an event, meeting or interaction. As a result of this lack of preparation, we are unable to respond to an opportunity quickly or effectively enough. Let me illustrate this with a personal experience:

As per my usual practice, I carried my iPad with me when I was invited to participate in a panel discussion being held during a literature festival.

One of my co-panellists was intrigued when she saw me quickly scanning through a list of points before the session. 'What are you doing?' she asked.

'Just reviewing some points I jotted on the flight,' I replied. (I often find that panel discussions, especially in the literary world, tend to meander. By reviewing the specific points I wish to make, I ensure that I stick to my topic.)

My co-panellist shook her head, convinced that I was from another planet. She had never come across an author who made notes in advance of a literary discussion! I had to be nuts!

It is often joked that the world is a stage and most of us are desperately unrehearsed. Imagine how the odds of your success could improve if you were rehearsed? Benjamin Franklin, one of the founding fathers of America, said, 'By failing to prepare, you are preparing to fail.' In a similar vein, Louis Pasteur said, 'Chance favours the prepared mind.'

Indeed, there are some people who can think on their feet. But they constitute a miniscule part of the population. For most others, it is planning ahead that helps. Consider this story:

Three fish lived in a pond: Planahead, Thinkfast and Waitandsee. One day they heard a fisherman say he would be casting his net in their pond the next day.

Planahead said, 'I am swimming down the river tonight.'

Thinkfast said, 'I am sure I will come up with a plan.'

Waitandsee said, 'I just can't think about it now. I'm tired.'

When the fisherman cast his nets the next day, Planahead was already further down the river and thus remained free.

Unfortunately Thinkfast and Waitandsee were caught by the fisherman.

Thinkfast quickly rolled belly-up and pretended to be dead. 'Oh, this fish is no good,' said the fisherman and threw it safely back into the water.

Unfortunately Waitandsee ended up in the fish market.

That is why people say, 'In times of danger, when the net is cast, plan ahead or plan to think fast!'

The eighteenth century British politician John Wilkes always had a witty comeback for any occasion. After a rival shouted that Wilkes would either die on the gallows or of venereal disease, Wilkes replied, 'That sir, depends on whether I embrace your principles or your mistress.' Game, set and match… it was a case of *think fast*.

But the inimitable Winston Churchill used to say, 'The secret of an effective "off-the-cuff" remark is that it has usually been prepared days in advance.' Once prepared, one simply had to file the repartee away in one's memory bank and listen carefully to decide when it would be appropriate to use: a *plan ahead* approach.

President Bill Clinton was famous for his 'extemporary' speeches, but he was always prepared. A snippet of a CNN report about one of his speeches confirms it:

'In his speech at the Democratic National Convention last night, Clinton still did just fine, just as he's done in so many speeches where he's treated his prepared text the way jazz greats soar from the sheet music.

'By one account, the former president spoke for 48 minutes and 5,895 words, while his prepared text, which was distributed beforehand to the media, was only 3,136 words. Reviewing each version, it's clear that the same person wrote both.'

Besides preparation, the other key element in the good luck harvesting system is planning and prioritization:

My friend and bestselling author Amish Tripathi wrote the first part of his blockbuster *Shiva Trilogy* and (like me) was unable to find a publisher. He met several industry insiders, some of whom asked Amish to edit or revise his manuscript, but he refused. He was convinced that his story would work.

His literary agent Anuj Bahri helped him publish the first lot of books and Amish paid personal attention to cover design and marketing. As of date, the series has sold millions of copies and is being made into a movie.

One day, I asked Amish how he had found the time to write his first book. After all, he had been an overworked banker in his previous avatar. How had he managed to juggle his work schedule to write the *Immortals of Meluha*?

Amish told me that his car ride from home to work and back took around two hours each day. He simply decided to use the time unavoidably spent in his car to get his writing done.

That's called planning and it makes a huge difference when an opportunity presents itself. Many people are so completely caught up in their disorganized and chaotic lives that they barely have a chance to do any of the things needed to increase opportunities, recognize them better or to respond to them. Examine the lives of successful people and you will see prioritization and planning:

Ghanshyamdas Birla is said to have loved lists. He had a list for everything, including one containing work maxims for his managers.

He also hated leaving anything unattended till the next day. A designated leather bag held his voluminous daily mail and papers, and he would go through them several times daily. He replied to all letters on the day they were received.

If you saw Mr Birla smiling, it meant that his leather bag was empty and that he had disposed of all pending papers and mail.

In my own case, I have found that a typical novel takes me around eighteen months to write, of which around nine months are spent on research. I used to regularly lose track of material (page numbers in books, passages that had been highlighted, web links, photographs or taped interviews) until I decided that all research material had to be linked, scanned or indexed to an electronic database that I could easily access. I asked a young techie to help me develop the database. That single decision made my research significantly more powerful and allowed me to allocate more time to writing and marketing my books.

It has rightly been said that planning can never be a substitute for initiative or judgment. But initiative and judgment requires free time. It is planning that frees up one's time. This includes planning one's finances, one's strategic goals and one's time.

I remember that in 1994, Margaret Thatcher visited Mumbai. I had been invited by my friends at Citibank to listen to her. 'Be on time,' one of the hosts requested. 'Why?' I asked. 'Nothing ever starts on time in India!'

'This is Thatcher,' replied my host. 'Even God is punctual with her!'

The chaps at Citibank weren't wrong. Lord Powell, Margaret Thatcher's private secretary from 1983 to 1990, described her as displaying 'excessive punctuality'. In an interview to the Guardian, Powell said:

> 'Her official car often had to pull into the side on approaching a town, because we were too early and

the police escort was not in place, leaving startled citizens wondering what the Prime Minister was doing in their local layby.

'The record was achieved on a visit to Prague, when she arrived early at the president's palace, whereupon the guard of honour snapped to attention and the band struck up the national anthems. Mrs Thatcher began to inspect the guard of honour.

'The only person missing was President Havel. He materialized a few minutes later, at the double and pulling on his jacket.'

Another trait of lucky people is that they leverage not only their preparation and planning but also their potential—their strengths. They identify opportunities by 'connecting the dots'. The following examples illustrate how lucky people leverage their intrinsic potential.

Take the example of Harland Sanders. One can see how a simple leveraging of strength was useful in attracting good luck:

Harland Sanders had a relatively successful restaurant and motel on US25 in Corbin, but when Interstate-75 opened seven miles from Sanders' restaurant, his revenues shrank. Given his knowledge of cooking, he began experimenting with a quick-cooking technique for fried chicken. He then started touring the country selling franchises of his new chain. By the time that he sold the business in 1964, Kentucky Fried Chicken (or KFC) had 900 restaurants!

Another example from the world of science and technology reinforces the point:

Jack Cover spent most of his career as a nuclear physicist. Leveraging his understanding of science and technology, he started a new company in 1970. He designed a weapon that could incapacitate assailants without killing them, and patented it in 1974. It was soon put into use by the Los Angeles Police Department to help apprehend violent suspects. When Jack Cover died at the age of 88, his device—the Taser—was used in over 45 countries.

In Indian business, an example that stands out for leveraging intrinsic strength is that of Sunil Mittal of Bharti:

Sunil Bharti Mittal became interested in push-button phones while visiting Taiwan and soon started importing them to replace the old-fashioned rotary phones then used in India. Having understood the phone instrument business, he entered into a technical collaboration with Siemens AG to manufacture electronic push button phones. Leveraging the manufacturing tie up, Mittal was soon manufacturing fax machines and cordless phones by the 1990s. In 1992, the Indian government began awarding licenses for mobile phone services. Leveraging his expertise in the telecom space, Mittal was able to secure a license and, eventually, become the largest operator pan-India.

A more recent example is to be found in the phenomenal growth of Flipkart:

Sachin Bansal and Binny Bansal, both alumni of IIT Delhi, were working with Amazon.com when they realized the need for an online price comparison site. The comparison site led them to an understanding of the size and potential of e-commerce in India. Starting with an initial capital of four lakh rupees (of which half was invested to buy computers and furniture) their new company Flipkart started off by selling new books, but today sells everything from apparels to consumer durables.

These are all instances of individuals leveraging their strengths. Why, that's precisely what John F. Kennedy did during his visit to France:

When JFK and his wife Jacqueline visited Paris in 1962, it was Jacqueline who stole the show with her fluent French. She charmed everyone, including

President de Gaulle. Just before departing, JFK called a press conference. He said, 'I do not think it is altogether inappropriate to introduce myself to this audience. I am the man who accompanied Jacqueline Kennedy to Paris, and I have enjoyed it!' Realizing that his strength in France was Jacqueline, JFK wisely decided to leverage her presence to maximum advantage.

Lucky people leverage preparation, planning, prioritization and potential. By doing so, they increase their ability to create opportunities or react and respond to them.

IV

Causing Ripple

In school we would use mnemonics to recall important study material. A mnemonic is a memory aid, often taking the form of a rhyme or acronym.

Going back to our rainwater-harvesting example, just imagine that it is raining heavily. You have placed a tub on your terrace to catch the rain. Each raindrop—or opportunity—falls into your tub *causing ripple* on the surface of the water.

Thus the best way of remembering all thirteen principles to good luck is by using the mnemonic *Causing Ripple*. Using this mnemonic, let's summarize the thirteen key attitudes and approaches that attract good luck:

C	Confidence	*Lucky people develop their confidence and communicate*
A	Alertness	*Lucky people find ways to remain calm and thus alert*

U	Unlearn	*Lucky people unlearn old attitudes and approaches*
S	Situations	*Lucky people make the best of bad situations*
I	Intuition	*Lucky people listen to their intuition and develop it*
N	Network	*Lucky people grow and strengthen their network*
G	Goodness	*Lucky people understand the power of goodness*
R	Risks	*Lucky people take calculated risks, cut losses, and learn from mistakes*
I	Information	*Lucky people stay informed and thus absorb new ideas*
P	Positivity	*Lucky people stay positive, persevere and cultivate a thick skin*
P	Passion	*Lucky people seek ways to get paid for their passion*
L	Leverage	*Lucky people leverage preparation, planning and potential*
E	Experiment	*Lucky people are willing to try new things*

These thirteen attitudes and approaches are by no means exhaustive. However, I believe they are the most common traits of people who eventually succeed in getting lucky.

When we examine the lives of lucky people, we may find one or more attitudes or approaches missing. We may ask, 'He's not a nice person. How did he get lucky?' or 'She's so disorganized. How has she been able to get anything done?'

Just as a student can compensate for a weak subject with a strong one, the same principle also applies to luck. The next chapter will explain how various attributes add up to a composite score, something that I refer to as 'the Luck Quotient'.

V

IQ, EQ and LQ

It is not unreasonable to say that we need some degree of smarts to succeed in a competitive world. The measure of human intelligence (or 'smarts') is known as Intelligence Quotient or IQ.

IQ is simply a number derived from a standardized intelligence test. Scores are calculated by dividing the individual's mental age by his or her chronological age and then multiplying that number by 100. So a child with a mental age of 15 and a chronological age of 10 would have an IQ of 150. In effect, IQ is simply the ratio of your mental age to your chronological age.

IQ stays quite stable throughout your life, so it is unlikely that a teenager with an average IQ can become an Einstein in later years.

Unfortunately we tend to associate IQ with success. That's utter nonsense.

During one's initial years, IQ is relatively important. Getting good grades in school or college, obtaining a highly paid consulting job at McKinsey

& Co, cracking a complex programming task at Google, or engineering a sophisticated derivative at Goldman Sachs does depend on IQ, but the importance of one's IQ begins to diminish as one advances in life.

Also, IQ is of little value in managing people, situations or relationships—critical factors in one's success. In that sense, IQ is a poor predictor of success. Realizing this, theorists came up with another concept: Emotional Intelligence. Emotional Quotient (or EQ) is a measure of this.

EQ is different to IQ. Instead of measuring your general intelligence, it measures your emotional intelligence. Emotional Quotient is a measure of one's ability to sense, understand and effectively apply the power and acumen of emotions to facilitate high levels of collaboration and productivity.

The five key drivers of EQ are self-awareness, self-regulation, motivation, empathy and social skills. It is not difficult to understand why EQ components play a more important role than IQ as one progresses in life.

Unlike IQ that cannot be improved upon, EQ can be increased. Developing a professional plan to strengthen your weak areas can (and does) improve your EQ. Increasingly, management experts have been coming around to the view that successful people are those who can combine high IQ with high EQ.

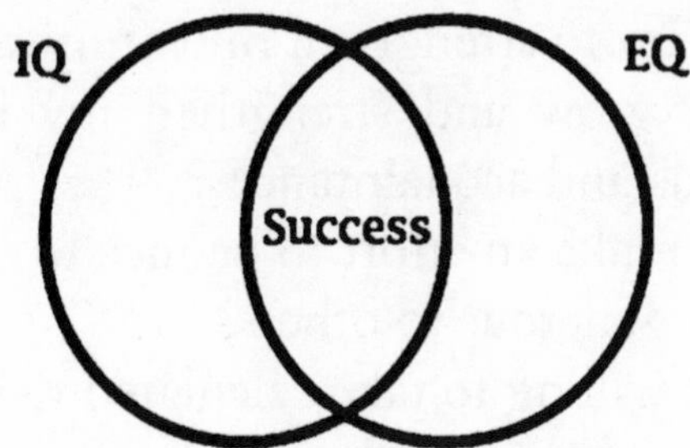

The problem though is that one can't simply explain success by correlating it to an overlap of IQ and EQ. There are instances where a person of lower IQ and EQ succeeds while another with higher IQ and EQ does not. What explains it?

In my view, the unknown variable is what I call Luck Quotient (or LQ). In the process of writing this book, I have become convinced that Napoleon Bonaparte was right. Being lucky is not determined by the heavens but by our ability to raise opportunities, recognize them, and respond to them.

Pause for a moment and ask yourself:

- Am I confident about myself?
- Do I communicate effectively with people?
- Do I stay calm, even in stressful situations?
- Do I remain alert to opportunities and developments around me?
- Do I try to forget old attitudes and approaches?
- Do I make the best of bad situations?
- Do I listen to my intuition?

- Do I try to strengthen my intuitive abilities?
- Do I grow and strengthen my network of friends and acquaintances?
- Do I make an effort to be nice to others?
- Am I generous to others?
- Am I willing to take calculated risks?
- Do I cut losses and quit when needed?
- Do I learn from my mistakes?
- Do I stay informed?
- Do I pick up ideas and absorb them for future use?
- Do I have a positive attitude to life?
- Do I persevere in the face of failure?
- Do I avoid getting affected when others criticize me?
- Do I seek opportunities to get paid for my passion?
- Do I prepare for situations in advance?
- Do I usually organize, plan and prioritize?
- Do I leverage my strengths and potential?
- Am I open and willing to try new things?

If you answered yes to most of these questions, the chances are that you have a high LQ. A high LQ is an indicator of your ability to attract good luck. If your LQ isn't too good, don't despair. You can work on your weaknesses and thus improve your LQ over time.

LQ is possibly the unknown variable that explains why some people are successful and others, probably with equally high IQs and EQs are not.

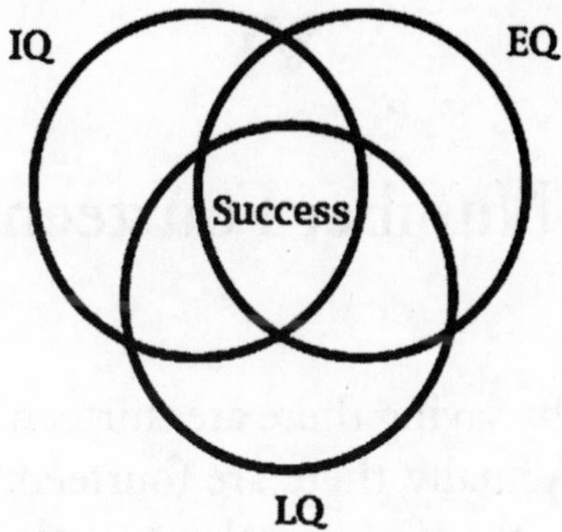

In effect, anyone can be lucky. The American politician William Jennings Bryan said, 'Destiny is not a matter of chance; it is a matter of choice. It is not a thing to be waited for, it is a thing to be achieved.'

In similar vein, Shakespeare (in his play Julius Caesar) said 'Men are at some time masters of their fates; The fault, dear Brutus, is not in our stars, But in ourselves…'

VI

Number Fourteen

I started out by saying there are thirteen steps to good luck. I lied. Actually, there are fourteen.

What is the fourteenth step that deserves a separate chapter?

In Chapter V, I suggested that successful people manage to combine IQ, EQ and LQ. In this sixth and final chapter I will try to distinguish between successful people and happy people.

At a very broad level, all human needs (or desires) can be lumped into nine basic categories:

1. Subsistence, e.g. food, shelter, clothing
2. Protection, e.g. social security or health insurance
3. Affection, e.g. friendships, family relationships, marriage
4. Understanding, e.g. education, reasoning, meditation

5. Participation, e.g. associations, community, neighbourhood, church or temple
6. Leisure, e.g. holidays, parties, sports
7. Creation, e.g. business growth, writing, music composition, art
8. Identity, e.g. self-esteem, public profile
9. Freedom, e.g. dissent, autonomy

Man has always thought that luck is about getting closer to fulfilment of one or more desires.

The problem, however, is that many have succeeded in having one or more desires fulfilled but continue to remain unhappy even after fulfilment. Can such people be considered lucky?

It has been said that success is about having what you want, but happiness is about wanting what you have. In effect, the fourteenth step for good luck is this:

Lucky people are those who are able to see how lucky they are.

In effect, truly lucky people are able to count and appreciate their blessings. This realization is the most important step to bloody good luck! You may not be doing too well at work, but still have a loving family and good health. Shouldn't you count those as blessings? You may have tripped on the road and skinned you knee but there was no traffic. Shouldn't you be happy that your life was in no danger?

Lucky people not only implement the thirteen steps to attract good luck. They are also able to objectively appreciate what they already have.

Let me narrate a final story to end this book on a fitting note:

A high-flying CEO from New York City arrived at a small village in Gujarat as a tourist. Seeing a small shop selling traditional handmade dolls, he decided to do some shopping for his daughters back home.

The shop was little more than a shack with a brass bell hanging outside near the main window. Seeing no shopkeeper to assist him, the American rang the bell.

After several minutes, the sleepy owner emerged from his living quarters located behind the shop.

'Yes sahib, how may I help you?' he asked, rubbing his eyes drowsily.

Somewhat irritated by the casual attitude, the American asked, 'What is the point of owning a shop if you are not around to assist your customers?'

'A thousand apologies, sir,' said the owner. 'This is a simple village. I sleep late, do a little farming, play with my children, take an afternoon siesta with my wife, and sit under the banyan tree each evening where I sip sugary tea and sing songs with my friends. The shop is only a small part of my life.'

The American businessman bought a few dolls, but couldn't resist offering some advice.

'I am an engineer from Stanford with an MBA from Harvard. I am the CEO of a Fortune 500 company. My business advice to you is that you should be standing outside the hut and inviting tourists into your shop.'

'And how will that help me, sahib?' asked the shopkeeper, wrapping the dolls in newspaper at a leisurely pace.

'You would get much more business. You could even double your daily sales,' replied the American.

'And how will that help me, sahib?' asked the shopkeeper as he carefully tied the package with some string.

'You will be able to employ sales people. Your revenues will increase and you will be able to open an automated factory rather than having to make dolls by hand.'

'And how will that help me, sahib?' asked the shopkeeper wearily as he handed over change to the American.

'You could start exporting dolls to the rest of the world. You would become a corporate entity with hundreds of staff members, fantastic revenues and a globally respected business,' said the American excitedly.

'And how will that help me, sahib?' asked the shopkeeper handing over the package to the American.

'When the time is right, you would announce an IPO, sell your company's shares to the public and become very rich. You would make millions!' said the American.

'And how will that help me, sahib?' asked the shopkeeper, stifling a yawn.

'Then you would retire and move to a small village of your dreams. You would be able to sleep late, do a little farming, play with your children, take an afternoon siesta with your wife, and sit under a banyan tree each evening while sipping sugary tea and singing songs with your friends.'

'But isn't that what I am doing already?' asked the shopkeeper as he headed back to complete his afternoon nap.

Acknowledgements

My sincere thanks to:

My publisher—Gautam Padmanabhan.

My editor—Ashok L. Rajani.

The team at ThinkWhyNot—particularly Sangram Surve and Shaista Madhani—for their brilliant cover design.

Vipin Vijay, for his efforts at perfecting the inside layout for easy readability of this book.

Krishna Kumar, Satish Sundaram and countless others at Westland.

My close friends—Apurva Diwanji, Sunil Dalal and Rajesh Jaggi—whose inputs were immensely valuable while developing the book outline.

My wife and son—Anushika and Raghuvir—for putting up with my absence while I wrote this book and several others.

My family—Manju, Vaibhav and Vidhi—whose ideas inspired many of the concepts in this book.

13 Steps to Bloody Good Luck was launched in August 2014 and since then has been on bestseller lists almost continuously. In March-April 2015, we organised a contest in which we asked participants to submit their own good luck stories. The thirteen best stories would be included in the 2016 edition of the book. Hundreds of entries were received but the ones that appealed most to our judges are presented right here.

Story: Luck Around My Wrist
Contributor: Soumya Bollapragada, Hyderabad

A chance meeting with Prince Manvendra Singh Gohil in a plush Mumbai hotel made me his *Rakhi* sister. We were enacting "Waiting For Godot" and I was playing Pozzo. I needed that one big face to launch my theatre group. My rakhi brother rushed to my aid and in stepped the glamorous writer Shobhaa De. I was excited and ecstatic as I had always looked up to her. The play was a thunderous success and the Applause—the name of my theatre group—refused to die even after many weeks. Literally! The news reporting, pictures and Shobhaa De's lovely comments about me and the play began trending locally. One such article was noticed by the well-known Tollywood director VN Aditya who was scouting for a female lead for his next directorial. It was to be spearheaded by the great movie mogul Dr D Ramanaidu. As they say, all good things knock on one's door all of a sudden. Yet again, two wish list items were ticked off into one project—working with VN Aditya and Dr D Ramanaidu. My life was galloping ahead and before I knew it, one thing led to another and another film *Chandamama Kathalu* happened to me. This film bagged the National Award for the Best Telugu Film 2015, even though I had a modest role to play in it. And now, many opportunities later, I am quenching my creative thirst by heading a team of Green Gold Animation—the creators of *Chhota Bheem*—where I write, conceptualise and create.

Story: Once In A Lifetime
Contributor: Anjali Khurana, Mumbai

14th February, 2010 was a Sunday and I didn't want to sulk. Back then, Valentine's meant something to me! So I travelled from Mumbai to Pune with Mitali to stay over for the weekend at Swapnil's who had had promised to take us around. We explored the Osho Ashram till the afternoon, ogled at the Fergusson College crowd, visited Shanivarwada and returned home at around four o'clock for a quick nap. The idea was to visit the German Bakery at around seven. We gulped a pint of beer each and crashed. Once Swapnil and Mitali were awake, I fell asleep yet again! I refused to go, I said, "I'm simply not up to it guys, let's not go to German Bakery today, let's stay in and knock back a few beers." They were pissed off but we called for more alcohol and drank into the wee hours. At around noon the next day, I opened my eyes to the sound of an agitated news anchor screeching over my head. A bomb blast had killed seventeen people and injured sixty in Pune's German Bakery at 7:15 pm the previous evening. The earth slipped from beneath my feet for a moment! I looked at Mitali and Swapnil, flabbergasted. They came closer, Mitali held my hand; Swapnil patted my back and murmured his heartfelt thanks. I was too dazed to react. I simply pondered over my luck—my Bloody Good Luck!

Story: Embrace the Lesson; Love your Life
Contributor: Shruti Mathew, Vishakapatnam

Days rushed by. Remaining jobless in the new city was a curse. Each morning as I sat on my armchair in my balcony, I often noticed people accusing an old beggar woman. They taunted her, telling her not to show her ugly face and make their day turn bad. I wondered, "Can someone's face give us good luck or a bad luck?" After a rather long struggle, I finally got a call for an interview. I badly needed a job. My parents were not healthy anymore. In addition, I needed to pay debtors. With many things on my mind, I rushed towards the bus stop and just then I happened to see the old beggar lady. It was just a glance, but I did not forget to smile. She too replied with a feeble smile. Confused and troubled with my thoughts I continued my journey. By God's grace and my parents' blessings, I succeeded in winning the hearts of the interview panel. Back home, I recalled the comments of the people on the lady and realised that she had been my good luck charm.

Story: Good Luck in Disguise
Contributor: Sangeeta Bhatnagar, Meerut

Eight years ago I was a teacher in a New Delhi school. It was nothing impressive but I was happy. In July 2007 my husband told me that we had to move to Meerut as he had been told by his company to head a business project based there. It meant I had to leave my job and shift to a small town. Although it was a great career opportunity for my husband, for me it meant a bump in my career. "What bad luck!" I thought, but there was little I could do. We shifted to Meerut and I started tutoring students in my Meerut home. I soon realised that awareness about various health, environmental and social problems was lacking in the students. Also many children in urban slums had absolutely no education. I started an NGO called the Jagriti Foundation. My students assisted me in this noble cause. Many doctors, teachers, lawyers and other professionals also supported me. We began conducting workshops, seminars, and awareness drives related to health, environmental and social issues. Seeing our determination and enthusiasm, multinational companies and media came to our support. As of date, thousands of children have benefited from our programs and our good work continues. Although Meerut was a new city for me, I am now well-known. But honestly, the satisfaction and contentment I get by seeing smiles on the faces of children that we work with is far more precious than the fame and respect that I have got. My life ended up getting a true purpose in Meerut. Indeed, moving to Meerut was good luck in disguise.

Story: My Little Bloomer
Contributor: Shaily Bhargava, Noida

"Monotonous" was the word that we often used in order to run away from our sophisticated urban life twice a month on weekends. We would go to my uncle's serene farmhouse. "School, college then office, my life sucks with mundane routine unlike yours, Payal. You are a free soul, no deadlines, no mailbox-clearing tension and nobody asking you to make it big." Payal looked at me with her little ambitious eyes and said, "But I want to be like you, Didi! School then college. You have everything—car, house, clothes and freedom because you're educated. Trisha Didi, you are lucky!" I pondered over her words. Was I really lucky? Could these material things really make me lucky? Payal was seven and had big dreams floating in her head. I often spotted her flipping magazines and trying to write on old newspapers. One day, I visited the tiny cracked muddy hut where Payal lived with her parents, brother and grandmother. They had nothing, absolutely nothing! However, she had three things in abundance—dedication, desire and the honesty to realise her dreams. The next day, I laughingly asked her, "*Tujhe bana doon lucky*? I promise to make you lucky, Payal, if you promise to sit next to me in this car without opening your eyes until I tell you to." And just like that, holding my hand she stepped out of the car in front of a school, overwhelmed and crying. I had convinced her parents to allow me to fund her school education. Payal sees me as her good luck charm. Actually she's mine.

Story: Luck Will Find Me
Contributor: Apurva Nikade, Thane

I don't remember the exact date but remember every ounce of pain. I had turned 23 that year, was an MBA aspirant and was at a good point in my career. But destiny had something else planned for me. One morning I woke up with severe back pain. I rushed to the doctor, underwent a few tests and all hell broke loose. I was diagnosed with Bone Tuberculosis. I sat there in dismay, blaming my bloody bad luck not realising that the real ordeal was about to begin—twelve months of heavy medication, medical tests and severe pain. I was a temperamental, impatient and anxious person and it was hard for me to come in terms with my situation. But then something changed within me. I began seeing my situation as an opportunity to change my way of thinking. I didn't know it then that I had started a journey of self-discovery. Those twelve months were really tough, mentally and physically. Looking back though, I discarded my temper and impatience and gained inner peace. Priceless! I'm 26 now and out of TB. I'm fit as never before and ran a marathon as well. I'm sure luck will find me one day. Till that time I'm just happy being unlucky!

Story: Lucky Thirteen
Contributor: Preethi Venugopala, Bangalore

My first conscious encounter with the number thirteen was when I was in college. During the farewell party, our head of department told us that we were the thirteenth batch to graduate from our college. Many sighs greeted this and we began to think that it was possible that our careers were doomed. Thirteen again made an appearance when I was engaged to be married on the thirteenth of June. This time it seemed like double-trouble, as my marriage was fixed for 26 September—thirteen multiplied by two! Time went by. My career and marriage progressed steadily. After marriage we shifted to Dubai and, coincidentally, my trip to Dubai happened on 26 April. I had by then decided that the number 13 was lucky for me. The curious number made an appearance once again when I successfully passed an interview for the Dubai Metro project on 26 September. I was overjoyed. When my son was born on 13 November, I thanked my lucky stars yet again. He has been the best gift God has given me until now. I am penning this story on 26 March and have a feeling that the number thirteen will prove to be lucky yet again!

Story: What Saved Us, Helped Us Grow
Contributor: Dr Praseena, Mangalore

1990. Friday evening. A holiday. Our weekly outing as a family. We then lived in Dubai. We all got into the car but I sensed something wrong. Terribly wrong. I told my dad there was a smell of alcohol coming from the front seat of the car. I looked at the driver through the rear view mirror and could see that his eyes were bloodshot. He was drunk. It was so terrifying. I pleaded with my dad. The smell was not just of alcohol. I smelt danger. My dad told me to shut up. It was like many other times when he would just ask me to put a plug on it. Around five minutes into the drive, on a steep hill, our driver revved up the engine and crashed head-on with a car coming from the opposite direction. Our car spun like we were on a merry-go-round. I looked at my younger sisters. One was ten and the other was just 13 months old. I looked at my parents gripping the seat of the car. We were hurtling towards a free fall of at least sixteen feet of darkness. And then the car stopped suddenly. A miracle! We ran out, took a cab home and prayed to Krishna. Prayed like never before, thanking our stars and our good luck.

Story: A Dream Job in a Dream City
Contributor: Amith Prabhu, Gurgaon

Social networks play a major role in connecting people and they work wonders if you use them, not abuse them. I work in Public Relations. Two firms were in talks with me to offer me a role in consulting in March 2011, one of which was Edelman—the world's largest PR firm. The windy city was a place I had come to admire after having visited it twice in 2010. I had neither dreamt nor wished then that I would work in this beautiful city. I was slated to be in Chicago in April 2011 for meetings and I had a couple of hours of free time on each of the three days I was going to spend there. So on a Sunday afternoon I visited the Edelman website, found the email address of the President of Edelman Chicago and sent an introductory email. I was stunned to see a response in four minutes flat and a meeting fixed for the following Tuesday evening. Unbelievable! Someone so senior had taken the trouble of responding to a stranger on a Sunday afternoon. I realised that there was a reason why it was the number one PR firm in the world. The twenty minute meeting went off smoothly and a few mails were exchanged over the fortnight that followed. There was complete silence for almost three months barring a couple of calls with HR in Chicago. Then on August 24th I got a call from HR in Chicago saying they had a job offer for me and that I should join within five weeks. My H1B visa application process would commence immediately. My credentials may have played a role in securing job in America but even today I think back to that one lucky email on a Sunday afternoon.

Story: Turning Point
Contributor: Raj Ahluwalia, Mumbai

I was 16 years old. My father was in dire financial straits and was searching for a job for me. I passed the IAF Apprenticeship Exams, but failed the medical. The doctor advised me to undergo surgery for Varicocele and join the batch commencing in ten days. Unfortunately the surgery turned septic and I was hospitalized for 17 days. The net result? I missed the batch. We could not afford to wait for the next batch so I got a temporary job as a civilian clerk in the local military office. I also began learning typing and shorthand. Four years later I secured a job in the Stanvac Bombay Refinery for double my salary. I worked and learnt on the job. I educated myself and earned a Masters in Economics. I garnered promotions and fifteen years later, I took over as Personnel Manager in Crompton Greaves and then as VP Human Resources in the Forbes Group. I was made Director of the fledgling Eureka Forbes and a dozen years later I was appointed Whole-Time Director in Goodlass Nerolac Paints and retired as Managing Director. Losing that apprenticeship was the luckiest day of my life!

Story: A Random Act of Kindness Can Change the Whole World
Contributor: Kashish Sadana, Ghaziabad

"Who is Kashish in this class room?" asked the voice. "Yes sir, it's me," I replied.

"Please take your bag and come with me to the principal's office," he said. "But why, sir?" I asked. "Because your parents have not deposited school fees," he said. "But sir, my father will deposit the fees next month," I pleaded. The class was giggling. "We will see to that later but at this moment you need to leave this classroom." I was in the fifth grade when my father lost his job and was not in a position to pay my school fees. I thought that I was the only unfortunate person on earth but I was wrong. The next day I heard the news about the earthquake in Bhuj, Gujarat. I wanted to help the earthquake-affected people by any means. I was good at drawing and sketching and so I, along with my father, went to the Sukhna Lake of Chandigarh and started the campaign for earthquake victims. I made more than a hundred sketches that day. I collected around two thousand rupees and donated it to the Prime Minister's Relief Fund. This small act of kindness made me into something of a star in the local newspapers of Chandigarh. My whole school applauded for me in the morning assembly and the best part was that I was given a scholarship for one year.

Story: Got Lucky with the President of India
Contributor: Sarath Babu S, Chennai

This incident happened in 2004. I was getting ready to relocate to another city and suddenly thought about sending my collection of poems to the then President of India, Dr APJ Abdul Kalam. I sent him my collection of poems—around fifty—and forgot about it. Almost a month later, I received a registered letter from Rashtrapathi Bhavan. I was speechless. Yes! It was from the Hon'ble President himself. What was truly amazing was the fact that he had gone through my collection of poems in substantial detail. He mentioned specific page numbers in his letter to me. There are thousands of poets in India. Most wouldn't imagine getting a reply from the President even in their wildest dreams. As Dr Kalam says, "There is nothing impossible in the world. Dream and only then you will be able to achieve it."

Story: Because it is Thirteen
Contributor: Ashwani Kumar Singh, Delhi

I am a football enthusiast and the game has been my passion since I was very young. My father was in the army and we travelled a lot but with his last posting just before retirement, we settled in Delhi. I joined the reputed Army Public School and wanted to become part of their junior football team in the sixth grade. I made my way into the team as a striker quite easily. Just before the first tournament of the year was to start, our coach asked us for the numbers that we wanted emblazoned on our jerseys. I wanted the number seven because I admired David Beckham—who wore the same number. Given that I was the new boy, I wasn't given that number and was allotted thirteen instead. I felt a little disheartened but carried on. I played almost all the games that year and scored in each and every match. I also ended up winning the Pele Award and the Sri Ram Singh Award during those years for my team. I eventually became the captain of my school's senior team four years later. Later on, I found out that there were many football greats like Michael Ballack and Nesta who also wore the number thirteen.